Moneywise

How to Plan Your Pension

1999 Edition

GW00692274

Other titles in this series include

Moneywise How to Save Tax

Moneywise How to Win on the Stockmarket

Moneywise How to Manage Your Money

Moneywise Guide to Buying and Selling Your Home

Moneywise

How to Plan Your Pension

1999 Edition

Keith Carlton

RD Publications Ltd · London

in association with

Prentice Hall Europe

London   New York   Toronto   Sydney   Tokyo   Singapore   Madrid
Mexico City   Munich   Paris

First edition published 1998
This edition published 1999 by
Prentice Hall Europe
Campus 400, Maylands Avenue
Hemel Hempstead
Hertfordshire HP2 7EZ
A division of
Simon & Schuster International Group

Every possible care has been taken to ensure the accuracy of the information
in this book, but no responsibility can be accepted for the consequences
of actions based on the advice contained therein. Readers are encouraged
to take relevant professional advice based on personal circumstances.

Editorial:
Brown Packaging Books Ltd
Bradley's Close
74–77 White Lion Street
London N1 9PF

Design:
Colin Hawes

Printed and bound in Great Britain by:
Biddles Ltd, Guildford and Kings Lynn

Library of Congress Cataloging-in-Publication Data

Available from the publisher

British Library Cataloguing in Publication Data

A catalogue record for this book is available from the British Library

ISBN: 0-13-011508-8

1 2 3 4 5   03 02 01 00 99

Contents

Ask the professionals   ix

Preface   x

1 Planning for your about tax   12

So what do I do?   16

2 Your lifestyle in retirement   24

Why you need a pension   32
The effects of inflation   33
The advantages of pensions   34
Divorce   35

3 Tax and National Insurance   36

Tax   37
National Insurance   42

4 Pensions from the State tax return   44

Basic State pension   45
State-graduated pension scheme   49

State Earnings-Related pension scheme 49

State benefits for widowers and widows 54

5 Introduction to employers schemes 56

Inland Revenue rules 59

Employers' contributions 65

Employers scheme benefits 68

How employers pensions are run 71

Eligibility for membership 78

6 Final salary employers schemes 80

How final salary is calculated 81

Early retirement 84

Other types of final salary scheme 85

7 Money purchase employers schemes 88

Benefits 92

Early retirement 92

Investment 95

Other types of money purchase schemes 95

8 More employers pension schemes 98

Schemes for company directors and senior staff 100

Unapproved pension schemes 102

9 Moving jobs 104

10 Personal pensions 112
Inland Revenue rules 115
Personal pension scheme benefits 125
Contracting out of SERPS 127
Special features 129
Other personal pensions 132
Should you have a personal pension? 135

11 Choosing a personal pension 138
Which type of personal pension? 140
Which type of investment? 142
Which pension provider? 144
Charges 145

12 Getting advice 148
Choosing an adviser – what should you ask? 151
How the adviser is paid 153
What should a financial adviser ask you? 154
The advice process 156

13 Checking your pension's progress 160
State pensions 161
Employers schemes 162
Personal pensions 166

14 Topping up your pension   168

Employers pension schemes   170
Personal pensions   173
Topping up a personal pension   174

15 Other ways to save for your retirement   178

Tax-free growth   180
When you retire   182

16 Taking your pension   184

Countdown to retirement   185
Pension increases in retirement   188
Should you take the lump sum?   189
Choosing your annuity   191
Tax when you take your pension   196

An A–Z guide to financial words and phrases   198

Directory   201

Index   204

About the **Money**wise Ask the Professionals panel ...

Throughout this book you will find comments and explanations from members of the Moneywise Ask the Professionals panel. The members are authorised professional advisers specialising in different areas of financial planning who answer Moneywise readers' letters every month. The panel aims to answer any financial queries. The service is free and using it puts you under no obligation whatsoever.

> For advice write to:
> 'Ask the Professionals'
> Moneywise
> 11 Westferry Circus
> Canary Wharf
> London E14 4HE

Janet Adam is a tax partner at chartered accountants BDO Stoy Hayward, based in Manchester

Walter Avrili is operations director at independent mortgage advisers John Charcol in London

Brian Dennehy is an independent financial adviser and managing director of Dennehy, Weller & Co in Kent

Kean Seager is an independent financial adviser and managing director of Whitechurch Securities in Bristol

Keith Sanham is an independent financial adviser at Fairmount Trust Plc, based in Leatherhead, Surrey

Rebekah Kearey is an independent financial adviser and a partner at Roundhill Financial Management in Brighton.

Preface

What are you doing with a book like this? It's not exactly light holiday reading, is it? Not quite a best-selling, unputdownable blockbuster, eh? But it is perhaps the nearest you'll get to something like that in the finance section of the bookshop. And when it comes to reading about savings, investments and tax, this has its advantages.

You can read it easily and quickly – because it's written in plain English, the everyday language you can use and understand. You won't lose the plot – you're taken through each section step by step and you get a recap at the end of each chapter. You won't confuse the names – we point out all the differences between a TESSA and an ISA and all those other financial acronyms. You can see what's going on – by looking at the many illustrations and charts. And above all, you get to read about people – people in the same financial situations as you (or at least like someone you know).

All the Moneywise books take this personal, accessible approach because your finances are personal – and money should be accessible. That's why we talk about 'you', 'your plans' and 'your savings' rather than 'certain higher-rate taxpayers', their 'schedule D tax' and their 'section 226 policies'. Of course, some financial terminology is unavoidable – but we make sure it's never incomprehensible.

But don't think that the jargon-free approach makes this book less authoritative than the weighty tomes beside it on the shelves. Our books are written by award-winning financial journalists, with advice from fully qualified and authorised independent financial advisers (IFAs).

That's why we think you'll enjoy a book like this. It has already sold so well that this is the second edition. It might not be unputdownable but it's always worth picking up. And while it's not everyone's idea of holiday reading, it could help you afford an even better holiday next year.

Matthew Vincent

Matthew Vincent
Editor
Moneywise

1 Planning for your retirement

"**P**ensions are boring. They take your money for most of your life, and the chances are you will die before you get any of the benefits back." "I don't need to worry about pensions – I will manage somehow when I retire. After all, the Welfare State will look after me in my old age."

Wrong. Most of the above is incorrect. The fact is that we should all have pensions to supplement the state provision – the old age pension – and that we should be planning today to provide for a comfortable retirement, free from constant worries about money.

PENSIONS AREN'T BORING
Well, not quite. It would be hard to argue that pensions are the most interesting topic: they are complex and subject to so many rules that it is difficult for anyone other than a pensions expert to understand them. However, most of the pensions experts have forgotten how to talk about pensions in plain English, and when we consult an expert we often come away more confused than before.

So pensions are boring-ish. But they are also the most important investment you are ever likely to make – more important than buying your house, and more important than life insurance and investment plans. A pension will pay you an income from the day you retire for the rest of your life, so you do not need to worry about your savings running out as you get older. But you don't have to worry – now – about planning your pension so that it will be sufficient for a comfortable retirement. See Chapter 2 to work out how much you will need to live on when you have stopped working.

WILL YOU MANAGE IN RETIREMENT?
Even if you save as you earn, and plan to sell your house and move to a smaller one to provide capital for your retirement, you are still taking on

a huge commitment. Your savings will be finite, and they could run out if you live longer than you expect. And who wants to spend their retirement calculating how long they have got before they either go broke or die?

The chances are that you will live longer than you expect. Better medical care, better housing conditions, a better diet and a better environment have all contributed to improving life expectancy in the UK and the rest of the developed world. In 1912, life expectancy was 51 years for a man and 55 for a woman. By 1952 these figures had increased to 66 for a man, and 72 for a woman, and in 1994, life expectancy was 74 for a man and 79 for a woman. In 1951 there were 271 people in the UK aged over 100. In 1997 the figure reached 4,400, and census statisticians predict that by 2030, the UK will have more than 30,000 citizens aged over 100.

A man aged 65 can currently expect to live another 14 years, and a woman aged 65 can expect to live another 18 years. This is a long period of your life to fund through savings alone.

A pension will provide for your retirement much better than savings ever can, but if your pension is on target to meet your retirement needs, you can use savings to supplement your income in retirement (see Chapter 15). The important thing is not to rely on savings alone.

THE STATE WILL PROVIDE

This is true but only up to a point. The State recognises that it has a duty to provide for its citizens in old age, but the state pension will not maintain your lifestyle in retirement. The basic state pension is worth around 18% of national average earnings. If you are earning more than the average, the basic state pension will therefore be worth even less to you.

Average earnings usually grow faster than retail price inflation, to which the basic state pension is linked. Even if earnings only grow 1·5% faster than price inflation, then by 2010 the basic state pension will be equivalent to only 14% of average earnings. By 2020 the basic state pension will be only 12% of average earnings.

To benefit fully even from this limited state pension, you need to have worked for most of your life. The maximum basic state pension – small though it is – will be paid only if you have paid National Insurance

Independent financial adviser and *Moneywise* Ask the Professionals panellist Rebekah Kearey says:

"The State cannot increase its pension provision and has decreased its commitment over recent years. The major political parties agree that there is not enough money to pay for increased pensions."

contributions for most of your working life (see Chapter 4).

Part of the reason for this is the problem outlined above – the fact that we are all living longer. This means that there are simply more pensioners alive in relation to the population as a whole. And since birth rates are declining in Western Europe, the proportion of workers to pensioners will continue to decline.

In 1985 there were 9·3 million pensioners. Ten years later, the number had increased to 9·8 million. By 2015 it is estimated that there will be 11·1 million pensioners, and by 2025, for every one pensioner there will be only two workers paying National Insurance contributions.

In the 1970s the State introduced an earnings-related pension scheme – SERPS – which replaced an earlier scheme, and was designed to provide an earnings-related pension for everyone. Within ten years of its introduction, the scheme was revised, reducing the promised benefits considerably (see Chapter 4).

In July 1997 the government announced that it was conducting a pensions review due to report in late 1998. The government's solution to the problem is the stakeholder pension. These would work in the same way that personal pensions do now, but would be simpler, more secure, more flexible and offer 'value for money'. The government argues that charges could be kept low because a government-backed pension – or a compulsory scheme – wouldn't incur expensive marketing costs. Stakeholder pensions might be available from unions, groups of employers and other providers, not just insurance companies. And some argue that there is no alternative to making pension contributions compulsory.

At the present time the government is considering what it calls a 'citizenship' pension for those millions of people who have to care for children or other relatives. You can only build up a pension if you're working, so these people miss out on the opportunity to build up a pension.

So what do I do?

The most important thing any of us can do is to start planning a pension as soon as possible. It is obviously difficult to motivate yourself to do that if retirement seems far away, but take a look at Chapter 2 to see why it is important to start planning now.

If you already have a pension, make sure that it is on track to meet your needs (see Chapter 2). If not, look at how you can top it up, so that it does meet your needs when you stop working (see Chapter 14). If you don't have a pension, you need to start one now if you can.

The box opposite gives the basic details of how pensions work – other than state pensions (see Chapter 4) – and the features they can include.

Your employer may run a scheme, and you should seriously consider joining it. Joining a company scheme is the best advice for most people who have that option – not least because your employer will contribute (see Chapters 5 to 7). If you cannot join a company scheme, you should think about starting a personal pension provided by a financial services company as soon as possible (see Chapter 10).

Throughout this book you will find clear discussions, written in plain English, of all the issues relating to pensions. You will also find examples to help clarify the points being made, together with checklists and flow-charts to assist your decision-making. At the end of each chapter you will find an action plan detailing the important steps that you need to take, and finally, there is a glossary at the back of the book for easy reference, explaining the technical terms used in the book, along with a directory of useful addresses and other important points of contact.

Your first stop should be the flowcharts on the following pages, which cover: planning your pension (page 18), getting the maximum for the state pension (page 19), boosting your pension scheme (page 20), making the most of your company scheme (page 21), making the most of your personal pension (page 22) and savings and investments to boost your retirement income (page 23).

These should help you identify the parts of the book which address any specific queries you have. But if you are starting from scratch, turn to Chapter 2 to work out what you're aiming for. Later chapters tell you how to get there.

Pension basics

○ Apart from pensions provided by the State you may be able to join a pension scheme with your employer or take out a pension, called a personal pension, from a life insurance company or investment management company. Pension schemes from employers are called either occupational pensions or company pensions. In this book we use 'employers pensions' or 'company schemes'.

○ Contributions to employers pensions are usually deducted automatically from your salary. You can make regular or one-off contributions to a personal pension.

○ You get tax relief at your top rate of tax on your contributions. In other words you won't have to pay tax on any income that you contribute to a pension.

○ You can contribute to a pension and get tax relief only while you are still earning.

○ A pension scheme may stipulate a retirement date, i.e. when you can start to take the pension. You may be able to decide a date that suits you, but it will not be before you are 50 unless you are in a certain type of occupation. There will be special rules if you do opt to retire early, or if you are forced to through ill health.

○ A pension doesn't just offer a retirement income. There are other benefits: it may pay out a lump sum if you die before retirement and provide for your dependants; it may provide a pension for your partner if you die before him or her during retirement; and it may provide a tax-free lump sum on retirement.

Planning your pension

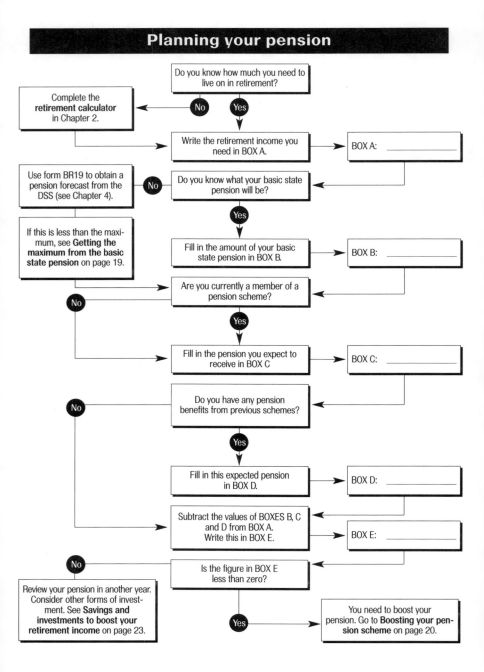

Do you know how much you need to live on in retirement?

No → Complete the **retirement calculator** in Chapter 2.

Yes ↓

Write the retirement income you need in BOX A. → BOX A: _____

Do you know what your basic state pension will be?

No → Use form BR19 to obtain a pension forecast from the DSS (see Chapter 4).

Yes ↓

Fill in the amount of your basic state pension in BOX B. → BOX B: _____

If this is less than the maximum, see **Getting the maximum from the basic state pension** on page 19.

Are you currently a member of a pension scheme?

No

Yes ↓

Fill in the pension you expect to receive in BOX C → BOX C: _____

Do you have any pension benefits from previous schemes?

No

Yes ↓

Fill in this expected pension in BOX D. → BOX D: _____

Subtract the values of BOXES B, C and D from BOX A. Write this in BOX E. → BOX E: _____

Is the figure in BOX E less than zero?

No → Review your pension in another year. Consider other forms of investment. See **Savings and investments to boost your retirement income** on page 23.

Yes → You need to boost your pension. Go to **Boosting your pension scheme** on page 20.

Getting the maximum from the basic state pension

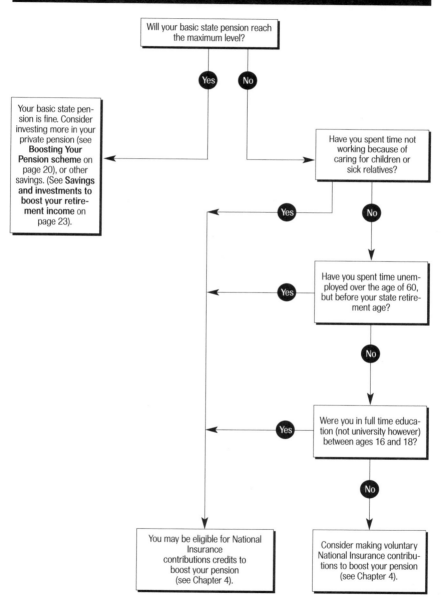

Will your basic state pension reach the maximum level?

Yes / No

Your basic state pension is fine. Consider investing more in your private pension (see **Boosting Your Pension scheme** on page 20), or other savings. (See **Savings and investments to boost your retirement income** on page 23).

Have you spent time not working because of caring for children or sick relatives?

Yes / No

Have you spent time unemployed over the age of 60, but before your state retirement age?

Yes / No

Were you in full time education (not university however) between ages 16 and 18?

Yes / No

You may be eligible for National Insurance contributions credits to boost your pension (see Chapter 4).

Consider making voluntary National Insurance contributions to boost your pension (see Chapter 4).

19

Boosting your pension scheme

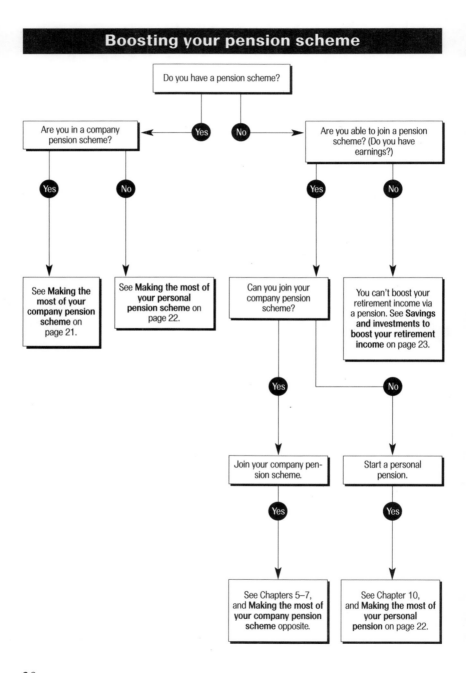

Do you have a pension scheme?

Are you in a company pension scheme? ← Yes No → Are you able to join a pension scheme? (Do you have earnings?)

Yes No

Yes No

See **Making the most of your company pension scheme** on page 21.

See **Making the most of your personal pension scheme** on page 22.

Can you join your company pension scheme?

You can't boost your retirement income via a pension. See **Savings and investments to boost your retirement income** on page 23.

Yes No

Join your company pension scheme.

Start a personal pension.

Yes Yes

See Chapters 5–7, and **Making the most of your company pension scheme** opposite.

See Chapter 10, and **Making the most of your personal pension** on page 22.

Making the most of your company pension scheme

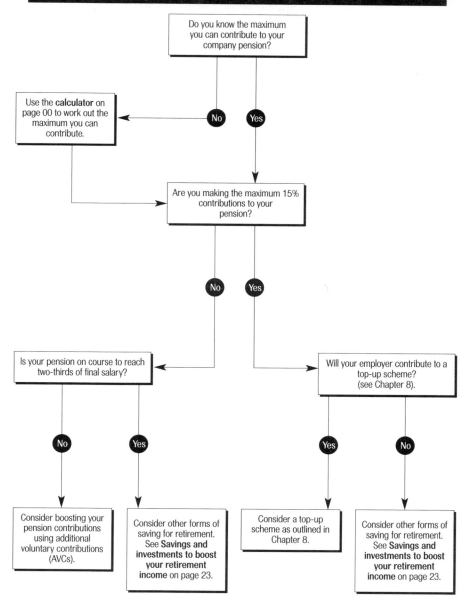

Do you know the maximum you can contribute to your company pension?

No → Use the **calculator** on page 00 to work out the maximum you can contribute.

Yes

Are you making the maximum 15% contributions to your pension?

No → Is your pension on course to reach two-thirds of final salary?

Yes → Will your employer contribute to a top-up scheme? (see Chapter 8).

Is your pension on course to reach two-thirds of final salary?

No → Consider boosting your pension contributions using additional voluntary contributions (AVCs).

Yes → Consider other forms of saving for retirement. See **Savings and investments to boost your retirement income** on page 23.

Will your employer contribute to a top-up scheme? (see Chapter 8).

Yes → Consider a top-up scheme as outlined in Chapter 8.

No → Consider other forms of saving for retirement. See **Savings and investments to boost your retirement income** on page 23.

21

Making the most of your personal pension scheme

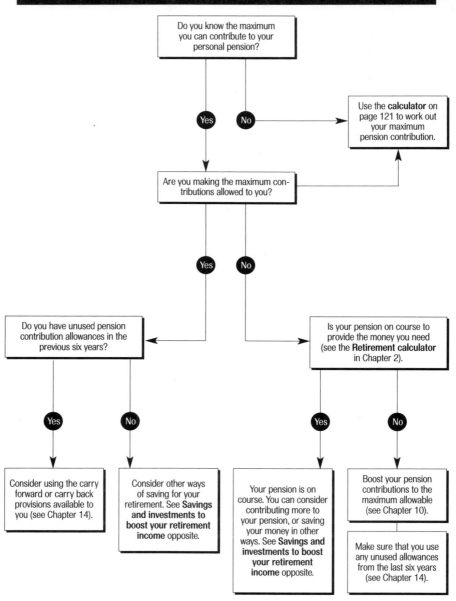

Do you know the maximum you can contribute to your personal pension?

Yes / No

Use the **calculator** on page 121 to work out your maximum pension contribution.

Are you making the maximum contributions allowed to you?

Yes / No

Do you have unused pension contribution allowances in the previous six years?

Is your pension on course to provide the money you need (see the **Retirement calculator** in Chapter 2).

Yes / No / Yes / No

Consider using the carry forward or carry back provisions available to you (see Chapter 14).

Consider other ways of saving for your retirement. See **Savings and investments to boost your retirement income** opposite.

Your pension is on course. You can consider contributing more to your pension, or saving your money in other ways. See **Savings and investments to boost your retirement income** opposite.

Boost your pension contributions to the maximum allowable (see Chapter 10).

Make sure that you use any unused allowances from the last six years (see Chapter 14).

Savings and investments to boost retirement income

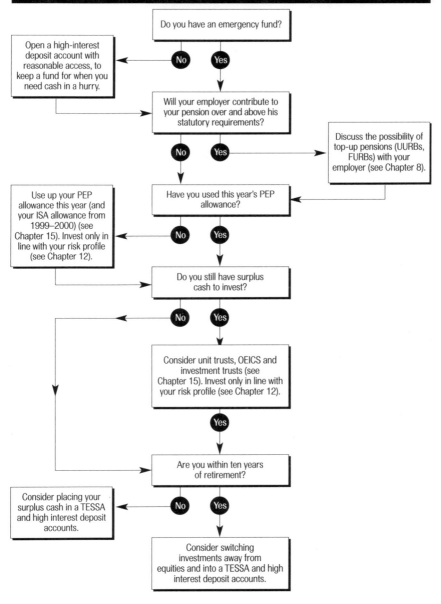

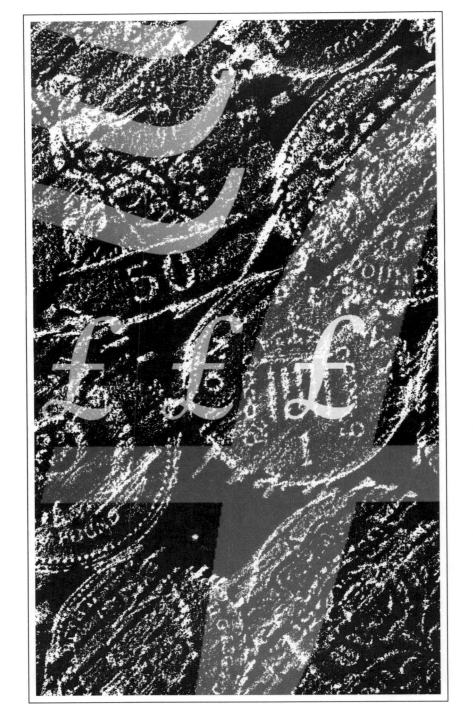

2 Your lifestyle in retirement

Almost all of us, if we are honest, will admit to thinking of our retirement as a future 'golden age' when the daily round of work will be behind us, and when all of our time will be leisure time.

Most of us have projects and ambitions that we postpone until we have the time and the money to indulge them to the full – whether it is starting a new hobby such as painting, or spending more time in the garden. Our families will be grown up, and may be living far away, so we plan to spend time in retirement visiting them. With all that leisure time we can take more holidays and see the world. And what is to stop us spending the winter somewhere warm, rather than in a miserable and wet UK?

Unfortunately, there is something to stop us – the lack of the money to do any of these things. Hobbies and holidays, even just visiting the children, all cost money. What happens if we do not have enough money? Worse still, what happens if we do not have the money to buy a new car when the old one finally breaks down (or has to go back to the employer which provided it)? What if we are spending our leisure time at home – but cannot afford to heat the house all day every day in the winter? And what if we are ill, and cannot afford simple changes to the house, such as a stairlift, which would help us to manage better?

It only takes a few examples to turn that rosy image of retirement bleak. But we can avoid the problems associated with having no money in retirement by starting to plan for retirement as early as possible. And if you aim to retire early you need to put careful plans in place.

WHAT IS YOUR TARGET?
The first thing to do is to work out how much money you really need in retirement. Once you have worked that out, it becomes the target you should be aiming at in your pension planning. You should do this even if you already have some pensions arrangements in place, then you will be

able to check everything is on course (see Chapter 13).

So how much income do you need in retirement?

SOME EXPENSES WILL REDUCE

You will not be travelling to work each day, so you won't need to pay the expensive costs of commuting, and you will not need a wardrobe of work clothes anymore. If you work from home, then your phone and heating bills may fall. If you have professional memberships, or subscribe to business magazines, those costs will reduce or disappear. Finally, in retirement you are likely to be free of other significant expenses:

○ If you are a homeowner, your mortgage is likely to be paid off, so the expenses of owning your home will reduce considerably.
○ Your children will probably be grown up with families of their own, so you do not have the expenses of feeding and clothing them, nor that of paying for their education.

OTHER EXPENSES WILL RISE

Sadly, far more expenses can be expected to rise than fall. Your fuel bills are likely to rise now that there are people at home all the time, and as you get older and less mobile you will start to feel the cold more. You may begin to need help around the house. Ultimately, you may have to install a stairlift or a downstairs bathroom, so you will need an emergency fund for these expenses.

If you have relied on a company car, you will have to be able to buy your own car, and pay the regular costs of maintenance, insurance and petrol. You are likely to become more dependent on having a car as you get older, especially if you retire to the country and cannot rely on public transport. With all this welcome free time, you will want to be able to indulge in your hobbies, and take extra holidays, particularly if your children live a long way away.

Finally, health issues grow in importance as you age. If you have private medical insurance, the cost of that insurance will increase as you get older. You may also have to consider the costs of long-term care, or of nursing homes, or both.

As a first step towards calculating your target, complete the retirement calculator on the following pages – it will help you work out the money you need to live on when you stop working.

The figure you have calculated is the net amount you need to live on in retirement.

Retirement calculator: part one

Your essential monthly outgoings in retirement

Remember that some of these costs will be lower when you retire, so put in an estimate of the lower cost. Some costs such as heating may increase, so put in a higher estimate than your current bills.

	Estimated monthly outgoings	Example
Grocery shopping (food, cleaning, toiletries, etc.)		£250
Rent or mortgage payments		–
Council tax		£60
Gas and electricity		£60
Phone bill		£25
Running costs of car (tax, petrol, insurance, AA/RAC membership)		£100
Other transport costs		£10
Clothing and shoes		£40
Dry cleaning, laundry		£5
Hairdresser		£25
Home maintenance (cleaning, window cleaner, gardening, repairs)		£30
Home and buildings insurance		£60
Life insurance and endowment policies		–
Other regular savings		–
Hire purchase or loan payments		£25
Other		£25
Total monthly outgoings		**£715**

Your pension is taxable. In the case of our example figures, if a single man aged over 65 needed £13,560 net to live on, the gross pension he would need would be £15,827. It is not immediately easy to work out what your pre-tax income needs to be – it depends on the personal

Retirement calculator: part two

Other non-essential outgoings
These are the 'quality of life' things, and not just the ordinary household expenses. This section should include the costs of hobbies and holidays in retirement. Try and estimate a monthly cost for this category.

	Estimated monthly cost	Example
Holidays		£120
Eating out		£60
Theatre and cinema, etc.		£30
Newspapers and magazines		£25
Drink		£50
Tobacco		–
Spending on pets		£25
Spending on the garden		£25
Birthday and Christmas presents		£20
The cost of hobbies		£20
Monthly savings for an emergency fund (to buy a car, put in a downstairs bathroom, etc)		£40
Total 'non-essential' outgoings		**£415**
Total outgoings (sum of Parts One and Two)		**£1,130**
Annual outgoings (12 x the figure above)		**£13,560**

allowances to which you are entitled, and the rates of tax applying to your remaining income. See Chapter 3 for more information.

You now have an idea of how much income you will need to maintain your present lifestyle when you reach retirement. Although this estimate is calculated in today's values, it is a valuable one because it gives you an idea of the necessary size of your pension in relation to your current salary. Assuming that your annual salary keeps up with the cost of living over the intervening years, you will need the same proportion of your salary to provide you with a suitable pension.

Example
The single man in our retirement calculator example earns £28,000 today, and the income he needs to provide for his retirement is £15,827 – 56% of his current income. As long as his target pension remains that proportion of his salary, he is on course.

NEXT STEPS

If you are already a member of a pension scheme, you can compare your retirement calculator figure to the pension forecast that your company scheme or your personal pension provides you each year. This forecast is based on your current salary or pension fund, and is a prediction of what your pension will be in today's terms if you remain in your scheme until retirement and make contributions at your current level. Compare the pension shown in your forecast statement with the figure you have arrived at in your retirement calculator. Will your pension be enough?

If the forecast pension is enough to meet your estimate of outgoings, then you are one of the lucky ones. Most people, unfortunately, are going to find that their pension will not be enough in retirement, unless they start to plan for the future now. Your calculations may show that you need to boost your pension. If you are a member of a company scheme, you can do so by making extra contributions called additional voluntary contributions (AVCs, see Chapter 14). If you have a personal pension you should increase your pension contributions to the maximum limit for your age (see Chapter 10), or make sure that allowances for prior years have been used to the full (see Chapter 14).

If you do not have a pension plan, either with your employer or personally, then you should start one now. You cannot rely on the state pension to maintain your lifestyle (see Chapter 4).

If you have not yet started a pension, look at the table on pages 30 and 31 to get some idea of how much you will have to contribute to reach your target income in retirement. The table is based on personal pensions only. It does not imply that you should take out a personal pension – if you have the opportunity to join your employer's scheme, you should almost certainly do this in preference to taking out a personal pension (see Chapters 5 and 10).

The table shows the contributions you would have to make each month to reach a personal pension of both one-half and two-thirds of your income by retirement age. All figures are in today's values. The table assumes that the pension will increase by 5% a year after you retire, but that it does not pay a survivor pension when you die. Investment rates of 6% and 12% are used to show the contributions you will need to reach

Reaching your pension target with a personal pension

Age	Salary now	Target pension % of salary	Maximum monthly contribution	Monthly contribution required	
Retirement age 65				6%	12%
Male 30	£15,000	50	£218·75	£187·84	£42·98
		66·67		£250·46	£57·32
	£30,000	50	£437·50	£375·67	£85·97
		66·67		£499·25	£114·64
Male 40	£15,000	50	£250·00	£269·42	£88·48
		66·67		£359·24	£117·99
	£30,000	50	£500·00	£536·40	£177·05
		66·67		£712·32	£236·08
Male 50	£15,000	50	£312·50	£459·00	£211·20
		66·67		£609·45	£281·61
	£30,000	50	£625·00	£909·00	£422·40
		66·67		£1,206·45	£560·37
Retirement age 65					
Female 30	£15,000	50	£218·75	£220·39	£48·26
		66·67		£293·87	£64·36
	£30,000	50	£437·50	£440·27	£96·53
		66·67		£584·21	£128·71
Female 40	£15,000	50	£250·00	£316·15	£99·39
		66·67		£421·43	£132·52
	£30,000	50	£500·00	£627·84	£198·80
		66·67		£834·31	£265·05
Female 50	£15,000	50	£312·50	£537·28	£232·16
		66·67		£713·42	£316·26
	£30,000	50	£625·00	£1,063·50	£473·19
		66·67		£1,411·30	£628·11

Table continued on next page

Age	Salary now	Target pension % of salary	Maximum monthly contribution	Monthly contribution required	
Retirement age 60				**6%**	**12%**
Female 30	£15,000	50	£218·75	£291·38	£73·50
		66·67		£388·53	£98·01
	£30,000	50	£437·50	£579·40	£147·03
		66·67		£769·50	£196·03
Female 40	£15,000	50	£250·00	£447·20	£160·08
		66·67		£593·15	£213·44
	£30,000	50	£500·00	£885·19	£320·15
		66·67		£1,174·63	£426·55
Female 50	£15,000	50	£312·50	£906·00	£451·10
		66·67		£1,202·75	£598·75
	£30,000	50	£625·00	£1,790·50	£893·00
		66·67		£2,374·74	£1,185·48

your target pension fund. This does not mean that your investment will grow by either of these rates – they are simply the rates which the Personal Investment Authority (PIA), the financial services regulator, has stipulated for illustration purposes.

The table also shows the maximum contributions allowable by the Inland Revenue at different ages. In many cases, the contribution you would need to be on target is higher than the contribution allowed. The figure has been italicised where this is the case.

As you can see, the later you start, the harder it is to reach your target pension.

Why you need a pension

You may think that you do not need to start a pension plan, and that other savings which you have will help to pay for your retirement. Or you may be planning to sell your present house and buy a smaller one in a less expensive area when you retire, to provide a retirement fund.

The truth is that unless you are an experienced investor with sufficient capital to play the stockmarket successfully, you are very unlikely to build up the kind of funds you need to pay for your retirement.

Look back at the annual income you identified in your retirement calculator. Then consider this:

Example
In the case of our retirement calculator example, a man of 65 can expect to live 14 years when he retires and would therefore need savings of 14 times £15,827 – a grand total of £221,578. If he lives longer than expected, he is in trouble!

○ The average life expectancy of a man at age 60 is an additional 18 years; for a woman aged 60, it is 22 years.
○ At 65, a man can expect to live another 14 years, and a woman 18 years.
○ At 70, a man can expect to live another 11 years, and a woman 14 years.

Multiply your retirement calculator annual income by the life expectancy which matches your gender and your expected retirement age.

The example, right, has been slightly simplified – the tax situation of investments is slightly different, and it does not take into account any gains in investments during retirement – but it does show what a monumental task it would be to provide for your retirement without a pension!

The effects of inflation

Inflation will eat away at your investments. Most building society and bank account interest rates barely keep up with the rate of inflation, so your capital is increasing in real terms only slightly.

The table opposite shows what happens to £10,000 invested in a building society account at 7·5% interest over a ten-year period when inflation is 4%. The first column shows how much money you will need in the future to be the equivalent of £10,000 today. The second shows the building society investment. The final column shows the value of that investment in today's terms.

Although your investment appears to have doubled to £20,610, inflation means that the purchasing power of your money at current day values is only two-thirds of that. In real terms your investment has increased by only 40% over the period.

Year	Equivalent of £10,000 today	Building society investment at 7·5%	Value of that investment in today's terms
0	£10,000	£10,000	£10,000
1	£10,400	£10,750	£10,337
2	£10,816	£11,556	£10,684
3	£11,249	£12,423	£11,044
4	£11,699	£13,355	£11,416
5	£12,167	£14,356	£11,799
6	£12,653	£15,433	£12,197
7	£13,159	£16,590	£12,607
8	£13,686	£17,835	£13,031
9	£14,233	£19,172	£13,470
10	£14,802	£20,610	£13,924

The advantages of pensions

Pensions have big advantages over any other forms of saving you make for your retirement:

○ you get tax relief on your contributions;
○ in a company scheme, your employer will also make contributions to your pension (this would not happen if you were putting money into your building society);
○ your contributions are pooled with all the other contributions in the scheme, so you get the advantages of investing in the stockmarket as part of a large fund. This maximises the opportunity for investment growth, and minimises the risk.

Another advantage of pensions is that the funds used not to be liable to tax themselves. However, this tax break was severely curtailed in the July 1997 Budget. Chancellor Gordon Brown abolished pension funds' rights to reclaim tax paid on dividends from investments in shares. As pension funds have large stockmarket holdings this has had a severe impact on their capacity for growth. Exactly how this will affect your options depends on what your pension plan provider has decided to do. It could be worth getting in touch to find out how your plan is affected and whether you should increase your contributions.

This makes it even more important to start a pension early or assess how your pension is doing. You may find you will need to make extra contributions. The Inland Revenue limits the amount of contributions you can make; if you are up to the limit, you may need to use other investments to make extra provision (see Chapter 15).

Divorce

One in three marriages currently ends in divorce. Women are more likely to have had an interrupted career, due to raising a family, for example, and are still more likely to be in lower-paid jobs than men, so there is a huge disparity between the pension benefits being accumulated by men and by women.

Independent financial adviser and *Moneywise* Ask the Professionals panellist Brian Dennehy says:

"If your pension fund relies heavily on dividends paid out by underlying investments for its year-to-year growth, there will certainly be a long-term impact on the size of your pension fund. Sensible analysts suggest a growth rate of 9% will fall to 8·25%, which means that someone with 20 years to retirement would need to increase their monthly contributions by about 8%. The precise impact will vary considerably from one pension fund to another, so it is vital for individuals to talk this through with their independent financial adviser as a switch of funds make be adequate to deal with the problem."

Men usually have better pension rights and, until recently, divorced wives were likely to have very little entitlement to income in retirement. The courts could make an order compensating the woman for the pension benefits she had lost through divorce, though this was only an obligation in Scotland. In England and Wales it was not automatic, and depended on the wife making a claim to the court.

The 1995 Pensions Act means that a court can make an order on the husband's pension scheme, which must pay the wife part of her ex-husband's pension when he retires. This is not ideal: the wife has to wait until the husband retires to have access to the pension benefit. For example, it is not entirely clear what will happen if the husband dies first. The government is reviewing the position and is expected to propose a clean-break settlement to replace the existing rules.

Action plan

○ If you have not already completed the retirement calculator, do so now, so that you know the target pension (in today's terms) that you require.

○ Compare this target with the forecast pension – also in today's terms – provided by your company scheme or personal pension provider.

○ If there is a shortfall, consider how you are going to make it up. Members of company schemes can make AVCs (see Chapter 14).

Personal pension holders can increase their contributions to the maximum limits allowed them (see Chapter 10), and use other allowances to make up for missed contributions in prior years (see Chapter 14).

○ If you are not in a pension scheme, join one if you can. If your employer has a company scheme, you should seriously consider joining it. Otherwise, start a personal pension (see Chapter 10).

3 Tax and National Insurance

Tax and National Insurance both affect your pension plans and your income in retirement, so this chapter gives a brief outline of how the systems work.

Tax

Although you can enjoy tax breaks as you build up your pension, you have to pay tax when you start to take it.

Income tax as we know it today was first introduced in the UK from 1799 to 1815, to pay for the Napoleonic Wars. The instigator was Pitt the Younger, and his resolution, in December 1798, met with great opposition. It was reintroduced in 1842, supposedly as a temporary measure, and is still with us today!

For historical and rather complicated reasons the tax year in the UK starts on 6 April, and ends on 5 April in the following calendar year. In this book, when you see '1998/99', this means the tax year beginning on 6 April 1998, and ending on 5 April 1999.

INCOME TAX RATES
At present there are three rates of income tax in the UK, which are applied in steps to your taxable income. The rates which apply in 1998/99 are as follows:

The first £4,300 of taxable income	20%
The next £22,800 of taxable income	23%
Taxable income over £27,100	40%

The 23% rate is considered to be the basic rate of tax because it applies to the widest band of taxable salary. The 20% band was introduced in the early 1990s.

PERSONAL ALLOWANCES

Each person has a 'personal allowance' – an amount of income on which you don't have to pay any tax at all. Other personal allowances are available, mainly for married couples and people who are over retirement age. Your personal allowance may be adjusted by the Inland Revenue if you pay tax through PAYE (see tip, opposite). This is to take account of over- or under-payment of tax, and also to take account of benefits you may receive from your employer which the Inland Revenue considers to be taxable, such as a company car.

For 1998/99 allowances are as follows:

	£
Personal allowance	
aged under 65	4,195
age 65–74	5,410
age 75 and over	5,600
Married couple's allowance	
aged under 65	1,900
age 65–74	3,305
aged 75 and over	3,345

Example
You are aged 70 and your total annual income is £17,100. Because you are aged between 65 and 74, you are entitled to an age-related personal allowance of £5,410. However, your income is £900 more than the income limit of £16,200.

You lose £1 from your age-related personal allowance for every £2 over the limit, so in this case your personal allowance is reduced by £450 to £4,960. You will be liable to tax on income of £17,100 minus £4,960, which is £12,140.

The higher allowances for people over 65 are available subject to an income limit of £16,200. For every £2 of income you receive over this limit, your age-related allowance is reduced by £1. Your allowance will not be reduced further than the basic single person's allowance or married couple's allowance.

So if you are under 65 you can have income of £4,195 before you pay any tax. A married couple is entitled to the extra allowance, but the tax relief is only at 15%, regardless of whether the taxpayer is a basic- or higher-rate taxpayer.

If you are employed, your personal allowance is indicated by the tax code that is issued each year by the Inland Revenue. It appears on your payslip, and also on the P60 you are sent each year. The P60 is a statement of your earnings for the tax year, showing how much tax and National Insurance you have paid. If you are self-employed, tax is not collected automatically. You have to make two tax payments each year.

Example

Each partner in a married couple – one 60, the other 55, is entitled to the personal allowance of £4,195. In addition, as a married couple they are entitled to the extra allowance of £1,900: this is initially allocated to the husband, though it can be split between the couple, or allocated entirely to the wife if preferred. To do this, use form 18 from the Inland Revenue, but you need to do it in advance of the tax year in which you want it to apply.

The husband in our example earns £20,000, and the wife £14,000 (they have no other income). In this case, the first £4,195 of the husband's income is entirely tax free. The tax liability on the remaining £15,805 is next calculated as normal:

○ The first £4,300 is taxable at 20% – a tax liability of £860.
○ The remaining £11,505 is taxable at 23% – a liability of £2,646·15.

This would give a tax bill of £3,506·15.

From this tax bill, the husband can deduct the relief allowed by the married couple's allowance of £1,900; at 15% this is £285. This sum is deducted from his tax bill, to give a net tax bill of £3,221·15. (If the married couple's allowance was given tax relief at his top rate, then he would only have a tax bill of £3,069.15.)

His wife's calculation is a simpler one. From her £14,000 income she deducts her own personal allowance of £4,195. This leaves her with an income of £9,805 on which she then has to pay tax.

Tip

It is important to check your tax code, which appears on your payslip and also on form P2(T) 'Notice of Income Tax Code'. Your tax code is an abbreviation of your personal allowance – it shortens it by missing off the last number. If your allowances total £5,200, your payslip should show your code as 520.

The Notice of Income Tax Code sets out your allowances and the deductions taken away from them. They should largely correspond with the benefits your employer has to inform you of using form P11D (or form P9D if you earn less than £8,500).

The letter which ends your tax code indicates your status: L for single, H if you have an additional allowance such as the married couple's allowance, P for a single pensioner, V for a married pensioner. There are other special codes, including K if your allowance is negative.

If you think there is something wrong with your tax code, notify your tax office, and make sure that you ask for an assessment of tax paid in previous years as well, in case you have been overpaying (or underpaying) your tax for longer than you realise.

Example

You are single and have a gross salary of £32,000.
Your tax liability is as follows:

		Tax due
Personal allowance of £4,195		nil
First £4,300 of taxable income	taxed at 20%	£860
Next £22,800 of taxable income	taxed at 23%	£5,244
Remaining taxable income of £705	taxed at 40%	£282
Total tax bill		**£6,386**

However, if you make a pension contribution of £4,000
in the tax year, it reduces your tax liability as follows:

Personal allowance of £4,195		nil
Pension contibution of £4,000	allowed full tax relief	nil
First £4,300 of taxable income	taxed at 20%	£860
Next £19,505 of taxable income	taxed at 23%	£4,486·15
Total tax bill		**£5,346·15**

HOW YOU GET TAX RELIEF ON YOUR PENSION CONTRIBUTIONS

Under the Inland Revenue rules, the income you contribute to a pension is deducted from your taxable income when working out how much tax you pay. If the tax relief were not available you would have to make pension contributions out of your taxed income.

When you retire and receive your pension, it is liable to income tax just like the income you received throughout your working life. All your income – from pensions, employment and other sources such as investment interest – is aggregated to calculate your income tax liability in any tax year (see Chapter 16).

TAX ON PENSION INVESTMENTS

Employers pensions and personal pensions take your contributions and put them into funds or investments – such as shares, cash deposits and other assets. All these investments are taxable if you hold them directly. But in a pension fund, some of the investments grow completely tax free. There is no income tax on the income that non-share investments produce, and no capital gains tax on the capital growth – i.e. the rise in value – that the pension investments achieve.

It's this tax-free growth that gives pensions the potential to grow faster than any similar investments – and produce a big enough lump sum to provide a retirement income.

Employers pensions and personal pensions were also free from corporation tax – which meant that they could reclaim the tax that was automatically deducted from share dividends they received. And because many pension funds did hold shares – to produce income and growth – this was a valuable tax break. Reclaimed tax was paid to them on a regular basis – it was called an advance corporation tax (ACT) credit. But in the July 1997 Budget ACT credits were scrapped.

Pension funds no longer have these tax credits to boost their investment growth. And as many funds still rely on shares investments for growth, pensions will be reduced. Some pension providers estimate that final pension funds will be 10–15% lower than they would have been with the ACT credits. How this will affect your employer's pension or personal pension depends on how your pension provider makes up for the loss of the tax break. Contact your pension provider financial adviser to find out how the change could affect you.

DEALING WITH THE INLAND REVENUE

The basic rules for establishing which is your tax office are:

○ If you're employed, your employer will be able to tell you the name and address of your tax office – if you move jobs, your tax office may change.

○ If you become unemployed you stay with the tax office relating to your last employer.

○ If you're self-employed or in a partnership, your tax office is usually the one nearest to where you work. If your income is from an employers pension, your tax office will probably be the one in the area where the pension fund office is. If it's only a small pension or your only pension is from the state, it will be the office in the area in which you live.

○ If your only income is from a personal pension, your tax office will be the one which covers the pension provider.
○ If your only income is from investments, then the office will depend on where you live.

Apart from getting help from your own tax office, there is a large network of Tax Enquiry Centres around the country. Any Inland Revenue office should be able to point you in the right direction. You can find addresses in the phone book under 'Inland Revenue'.

If you are making contributions to an employers pension scheme, you do not need to include any information about it on your tax return, unless you have made a lump sum contribution to an additional voluntary contribution scheme (see Chapter 14). If you're contributing to a personal pension you will need to supply information about those contributions on your tax return.

National Insurance

The National Insurance Fund is designed to pay for the state benefits administered by the Department of Social Security (DSS), such as unemployment and sickness benefits and state pensions. What you pay over your working life affects the state pension you will get.

All earnings from employment are liable to National Insurance contributions; income from other sources (such as investment interest) is not. Income from your pension is not liable for National Insurance contributions, even though you may have to pay income tax on that pension. Anyone earning more than a certain amount has to pay National Insurance contributions on their income. Employers also have to pay National Insurance contributions on behalf of their employees; these are divided into four classes:

○ Class 1 is the most common, and applies to employees and their employers. Employees pay 'primary' contributions and employers pay 'secondary' contributions. See below for details.
○ Class 2 is paid by self-employed people, and is a flat rate contribution of £6·35 a week in 1998/99, unless you earn less than £3,590 a year.
○ Class 3 is a voluntary contribution that you can choose to pay if you are not earning or have an interrupted National Insurance contribu-

tions record. The rate for 1998/99 is £6·25 a week.

O Class 4 contributions are also payable by self-employed people. If you have profits of between £7,310 and £25,220 in 1998/99, you are liable to pay Class 4 contributions of 6% of those profits.

Class 1 contributions depend on how much you earn, and whether or not you are 'contracted out' of the State Earnings-Related Pension Scheme (SERPS) – see Chapter 4. They are also governed by something called 'middle band earnings'. Middle band earnings are your earnings between the 'lower earnings limit' and the 'upper earnings limit'. In 1998/99, the lower earnings limit is £64 a week (£3,328 a year). The upper earnings limit is £485 a week (£25,220 a year).

If you earn less than £64 a week you do not pay National Insurance contributions. If you earn more than £64 a week you pay:

O 2% of the first £64 a week.

O 10% of the middle band earnings between the lower and the upper earnings limits. This is reduced to 8·4% of middle band earnings if you are contracted out of SERPS (see Chapter 4).

O No contributions for salary above the upper earnings limit.

Employers also pay National Insurance contributions. Their contribution scale is more complicated, depending on the type of pension scheme used to contract out of SERPS. Unlike employee contributions, employers have to contribute in respect of all the salary earned, unless the employee earns less than £64 a week. From April 1999, employees will pay no National Insurance contributions on earnings up to the lower earnings limit, however much they earn. Contributions paid by employers are also being changed from that date.

Action plan

O If you have not checked your tax code, do so. If you believe that it is incorrect, contact your tax office and tell them why you think the code is wrong. Check the tax you have paid in previous years as well.

O Check that you are receiving all the allowances to which you are entitled.

O If you think your National Insurance record is incomplete, enquire about making voluntary contributions.

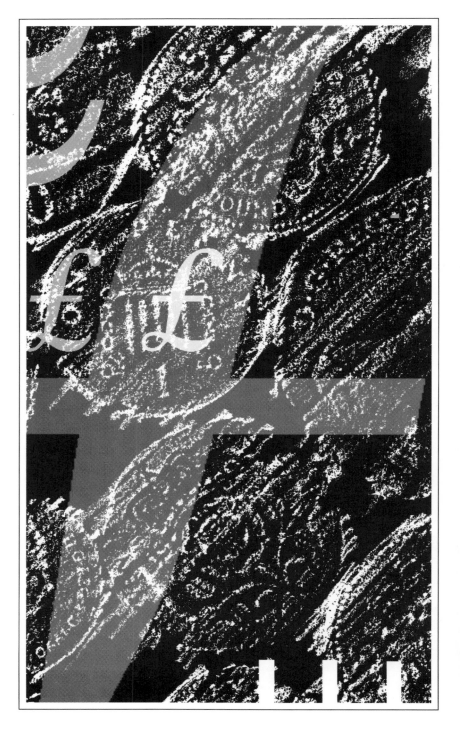

4 Pensions from the State

Since the introduction of the Welfare State just after the Second World War, we have come to think of the government as providing for us throughout our lives.

Yet while it is true that the State will always provide something it is essential to remember that what the State can provide is limited.

The pressures we talked about in Chapter 1 – especially the increased proportion of pensioners to workers – mean that provision can be expected to become less and less. As you will see in this chapter, the government has already had to scale back the benefits projected under the State Earnings-Related Pension Scheme (SERPS), a scheme which only began in 1978.

It is important to remember that the pension you can expect from the State is likely to play little part in your retirement funding. There are three types of state pension:

○ The basic state pension.
○ The graduated pension scheme.
○ SERPS.

Basic state pension

Everyone who has paid sufficient National Insurance contributions is entitled to the basic state pension. To receive the full basic pension, you need to have paid National Insurance contributions for at least 90% of your working life.

Working life means 49 years for a man, and, currently, 44 years for a woman. However, the rules for women are changing (see page 48).

You can be credited with National Insurance contributions for periods when you did not work, for any of the following reasons:

○ If you claimed job seekers' allowance, incapacity or maternity benefit.

○ If you are an unemployed man aged 60 or over, or an unemployed woman aged over 60, but not yet at your state retirement age (see page 48).

○ If you take time off work to raise a family or look after an elderly or sick relative, but only if you claim a state benefit for that period (such as the Invalid Care Allowance).

○ If you were born after April 1957, you can be credited with National Insurance contributions for time spent at school or on an approved training scheme between the ages of 16 and 18. Time spent at university does not count for credits.

> To find out what your likely entitlement to the basic state pension will be at retirement age, you can use the forecast service provided by the Department of Social Security (DSS). Pick up a form BR19 'Request for a Retirement Pension Forecast' from your local DSS or Benefits Agency office. The DSS will then send you a forecast of what it thinks you will be entitled to, based on your earnings record to date. It will also send information on how you can boost this, if necessary, through voluntary contributions. For more details see Chapter 13.

If you have not paid National Insurance contributions for the necessary period, then your basic state pension will be scaled down according to the length of time you have paid contributions. If you have not paid any National Insurance contributions, then you are not entitled to a basic state pension, and you will have to rely on other state benefits instead.

HOW MUCH IS IT WORTH?

In 1998/99 the full basic state pension is worth only £64·70 a week – or £3,364·40 a year. Married couples are entitled to an additional pension of £38·70 a week, provided that the husband has paid enough National Insurance contributions to qualify for the full basic pension.

A wife who has sufficient National Insurance contributions in her own right will qualify for her own basic state pension. This has the effect of 'topping up' the additional married couple's pension – up to a maximum equivalent to two single pensions.

> Independent financial adviser and *Moneywise* Ask the Professionals panellist Rebekah Kearey says:
>
> "Governments have altered the state pension system regularly ever since it began in 1948 because the cost of providing for the State's pensioners, in the manner that was intended, has proved too expensive for the country to maintain."

Example

Both husband and wife are retired, and entitled to the basic state pension. The husband qualifies for the maximum pension of £64.70 a week. The couple is also entitled to the married couple's pension of £38.70 – taking their income to £103.40 a week.

The wife, however, has paid National Insurance contributions for most of her working life. On the basis of this contribution record, she qualifies for a pension of £56.72. This is more than the married couple's pension, so effectively it replaces it. The maximum pension for the couple will be £121.42 (£64.70 + £56·72).

On the other hand, if she was entitled in her own right only to a basic state pension of say £25·00, then the couple would still qualify for the whole of the married couple's pension on top of the husband's pension. Their total pension would remain at £103.40.

Independent financial adviser and *Moneywise* Ask the Professionals panellist Kean Seager says:

"Do remember that the state pension increases in line with the retail price index. But the RPI usually increases more slowly than average earnings and of course your own spending pattern may well increase at a faster or slower rate than prices in general."

Remember that this will only happen if the wife has enough National Insurance contributions.

For pensioners aged 80 and over, there is an additional pension worth 25p a week. This is not indexed in line with inflation – in fact it has not changed since 20 September 1971! Pensioners also receive a £10 Christmas bonus: again this is not indexed, and has been the same since 1983.

The basic state pension is increased in line with the retail price index (RPI); the adjustment happens in April every year, but is based on the changes that have taken place in the RPI over the 12 months ending at the previous September.

Look back at the sets of calculations of your anticipated expenditure you made using the retirement calculator in Chapter 2. Even with the normal reduction in regular outgoings you can expect when you retire, the basic state pension – a maximum of £64.70 a week – does not go far. So the most important thing to remember is that you should be putting money into other pension plans, in order to boost your income when you retire.

WHEN YOU CAN TAKE THE STATE PENSION

For men the answer is simple; they qualify for the state pension at 65. For women the picture is now rather complicated. Women used to qualify at 60; however, the last government legislated to equalise pension ages for both men and women at 65.

This will not mean that all women have to work the extra five years before being able to take their pension, though. The change is being phased in as follows:

○ If you were born on or before 5 April 1950, you will still be able to take the state pension at 60.
○ If you were born after 5 March 1955, you qualify at 65.
○ In between, there is a stepped scale. If you fall into this category, you can work out the age at which you qualify as follows:
   ● count the number of months between 5 April 1950 and your own date of birth.
   ● a month for this calculation begins on the 6th of one month, and ends on the 5th of the next. A part month counts as a whole month.
   ● your new retirement date will be this number of months following your 60th birthday.

The important thing to remember is that there are no options for early retirement for anybody with the state pension. So if you are planning to retire earlier than the ages specified in the state scheme, it is important to look at other forms of pension provision or sources of income.

THE TAX RULES FOR STATE PENSIONS

When you receive your pension it is liable to income tax. If it is your only source of income, it should be more than offset by your personal allowance. If you have other

> **Example**
> If you are a woman who was born on 15 June 1952, there are 26 full months (6 April 1950 to 5 June 1952), and one part month (6 June 1952–15 June 1952). The part month counts as a whole month, so you should add 27 months to the age of 60. The age at which you qualify for the basic state pension is therefore 62 years and 3 months.

> **Tip**
> Your entitlement to the basic state pension is not affected by any other pensions you may have. But beware – if you are in a company scheme, its benefits may have been reduced to take into account your entitlement to a state pension. See Chapter 5.

income besides the basic state pension, all of your income is taken into account to calculate how much tax you owe, including your basic pension.

State graduated pension scheme

This was an early attempt at providing an extra pension that was earnings related, on top of the basic state pension. It existed from 1961 until 1975, and was replaced three years later by SERPS (see below).

The graduated pension scheme worked on a system of 'pension units' that were built up through earnings-related contributions. If you had contributed the maximum allowed under the scheme whilst it lasted, you would be entitled to a few pounds extra pension each week on retirement. Because many employers' schemes were considered to be adequate substitutes for the graduated pension scheme, many people were not required to make contributions to this scheme. Retirement ages were the same as the basic state pension.

If you did contribute, or are uncertain, then request a pension forecast from the DSS, using form BR19 (see page 46).

State Earnings-Related Pension Scheme

Like the graduated pension scheme, SERPS was designed to be an add-on to the basic state pension, providing an earnings-related pension. The legislation for SERPS was passed in 1975, although the scheme only began in 1978. Like the basic state pension, it is paid for through National Insurance contributions.

Only employed people are eligible for SERPS; the self-employed are excluded. Retirement ages are the same as those for the basic state pension.

The original scheme was modified in the Social Security Act 1986, because the government believed that the scheme as it originally stood would become too expensive to maintain early in the 21st century. These changes will affect people retiring in 1999/2000 and beyond. See below for details.

SERPS BENEFITS

Those retiring before 1999/2000

If you retire before the 1999/2000 tax year, SERPS will pay a pension of 1·25% of your 'middle band earnings' (the difference between the National Insurance lower and upper earnings limits – see Chapter 3 for details) for each year you contributed to SERPS between 1978 and 1999. This would give you a maximum pension of 25% of your middle band earnings. Middle band earnings for a given year are increased in line with the increase in national average earnings for the time between that year and the year of retirement.

Those retiring in 1999/2000 or later

For those in this group, the original promise of SERPS was a pension of 25% of the average of their best 20 years' middle band earnings – revalued in line with increases in national average earnings. However, this was the area of SERPS which suffered in the 1986 changes. Rather than being an average of the best 20 years' middle band earnings, the calculation is now based on an average of your lifetime earnings, but still revalued, of course. This has the effect of reducing the size of your SERPS pension, since in the early years of our working lives, most of us earn a considerable amount less than in later years. On top of this change, the percentage of middle band earnings that will be paid is being reduced over ten years from 25% to 20% (see table).

For anyone contributing towards a SERPS pension, there are two important things to remember:

○ The upper earnings limit (the top of your middle band earnings) does not increase in line with average earnings, but in line with increases in the RPI, which are generally lower, so middle band earnings are not keeping up with national

Tax year in which state pension age falls	% middle band earnings
2000/01	24·5%
2001/02	24%
2002/03	23·5%
2003/04	23%
2004/05	22·5%
2005/06	22%
2006/07	21·5%
2007/08	21%
2008/09	20·5%
2009/10 (and after)	20%

average wages.

○ Any income higher than the upper earnings limit is ignored by SERPS, so for those earning more than £25,220 a year a significant proportion of income falls outside the SERPS provisions.

FURTHER CHANGES TO SERPS

An additional change to SERPS relates to the method of calculating the middle band earnings, and again this change does not apply to all members of SERPS. It will apply only to those retiring on or after 6 April 2000 (unlike the above changes, which affect people retiring from 6 April 1999).

Currently the system works as follows:

○ The government takes your earnings in a given year up to the upper earnings limit, and revalues them in line with increases in average earnings for the years up to retirement date.

○ It then takes the lower earnings limit for the year in question, and revalues that up to the retirement date – in line with increases in the RPI. This 'revalued lower limit' is then deducted from the figure calculated in step one, to give the 'revalued middle band earnings'.

> **Tip**
> It is not easy to calculate the value of a SERPS pension yourself. The best method is to use the pensions forecast service provided by the DSS. To do this, complete form BR19, which is available from your local DSS or Benefits Agency office.

Under the new system – starting from 6 April 2000 – both the lower limit and the upper limit will be revalued in line with national average earnings, which generally increase faster than the RPI. This will mean that the calculation of your middle band earnings will be smaller than under the old system because the lower limit will be moving faster than before, which means that you qualify for a smaller SERPS pension.

One other change may help improve your pension slightly. If you retire after 6 April 2000, your SERPS pension is calculated on the best 44 years of your working life, and not the full 49 years the State assumes.

CONTRACTING OUT OF SERPS

You are allowed to 'contract out' of SERPS if you are a member of a suitable employers pension scheme or if you have a personal pension set up for the purpose of receiving the SERPS pension contributions. Contracting out means that you don't pay into the SERPS pension. Instead, your employers pension or personal scheme must provide benefits to match those which SERPS would have provided. Both you and your employer are eligible for a rebate on National Insurance contributions, in return for your pension compensating for the SERPS benefits.

Contracting out with an employers scheme
The Pensions Act 1995 defined a suitable employers pension scheme as being one which offers a pension for each year of service of at least 1/80 of 90% of middle band earnings. This is considerably less than most schemes offer. In addition, the scheme must offer a survivor pension of 50% of the member's pension, and the pension must be increased in line with the 'limited prices index' (LPI).

The LPI is a measure that came into effect in April 1997. It means that the pension increases each year in line with the RPI, but with a 5% cap on the increase. So, if the RPI is 7%, your pension increase would be limited to 5%.

If you are a member of a final salary employers pension scheme (see Chapter 6), then the rebate for opting out of SERPS is 1·6% of National Insurance contributions on middle band earnings for the employee, and 3% of National Insurance contributions for the employer. If you are a member of a money purchase occupational pension scheme (see Chapter 7), then the rebate is age-related from 1997/98 onwards.

Contracting out with a personal pension
Most employers pension schemes are already contracted out of SERPS. If you are a member of one which is not contracted out, and you would like to contract out, then you can, using an appropriate personal pension scheme set up for that purpose only. The money you and your employer save in National Insurance contributions is credited by the DSS to the pension provider.

If you opt for a personal pension because an employers pension is not available in your case, or you decide a personal pension is a better option for you, you can also use an appropriate personal pension to contract out. The appropriate personal pension will exist alongside the personal pension plan which is funded by your own contributions. The rebate for contracting out to a suitable

> An appropriate personal pension scheme is one which satisfies the Inland Revenue's requirements on contracting out. It can only hold the National Insurance contributions rebates from the DSS.

personal pension is again age-related from 1997/98 onwards (see Chapter 10).

The impact of contracting out
If you contract out of SERPS through your company scheme or through a personal pension, then those schemes are required to provide certain benefits, to ensure that you do not lose financially as a result of contracting out. The protections required are that the schemes pay a pension similar to the one which would have been built up in SERPS. This pension has to increase each year, and it has to pay survivor pensions.

How the protections apply depends on the type of pension scheme used to contract out. More details can be found in Chapter 5 and Chapter 10. Remember that these protections apply only to the part of your pension which is equivalent to what you would have been entitled to under SERPS. Your company scheme or personal pension will usually provide benefits in excess of those requirements in any case.

Who should contract out?
The reason for contracting out should be that the National Insurance contributions rebate for a particular tax year produce a pension larger than the amount of pension which SERPS would have provided.

Whether or not an individual should contract out of SERPS is a complicated decision, and largely depends on the age and sex of each individual. In addition, age-related rebates are being changed from April 1999 and this has altered the previous assumptions about whether or not to contract out for members of certain types of pension scheme.

Chapters 5, 6 and 7 will discuss the contracting out decision in relation to employers pension schemes, and Chaper 10 covers contracting out with respect to personal pensions. But if you are considering contracting out of SERPS, then your first step should be to discuss the matter with an independent financial adviser. Chapter 12 provides help with finding a pensions adviser.

> **Be Aware!**
> If you are already contracted out of SERPS, there may be grounds for contracting back in – where the National Insurance contributions rebate begins to lose its potential for exceeding the SERPS pension.
> You should consult a qualified independent financial adviser.

State benefits for widowers and widows

WIDOWERS

A husband whose wife dies cannot expect any state pension as a result of his wife's death, unless his wife died when both she and her husband were over the state pension age, and if the husband had given up working; in this case he would be entitled to any SERPS pension which she received. However, this will change: if the wife dies after 5 April 2000, he will only receive half her SERPS pension.

A widower with dependent children can have extra tax-free income through the additional personal allowance. This is an allowance for single parents with dependent children – children under 16, or children over 16 who are in full-time education. The allowance is £1,900 in the 1998/99 year, but relief is given at only 15%, in the same way as the married couple's allowance (see Chapter 3).

WIDOWS

All widows are entitled to extra tax-free income through the widow's bereavement allowance (£1,900 in 1998/99); this is also restricted to tax relief at 15%. This allowance is given to the widow in the year of bereavement, and also in the following year if she has not remarried. Widows with dependent children are also entitled to the additional personal allowance.

The state pension system treats widows differently depending on their age at the time of their husband's death:

Widows aged between 55 and their state pension age
If you are in this age band when your husband dies, you are entitled to the same basic state pension to which he would have been entitled. This would be the full pension of £64.70 if he had paid sufficient National Insurance contributions over his working life.

When you reach your own state pension age – between 60 and 65 depending on your birth date – you can choose to stay on your widow's pension until 65, or take your own basic state pension. This will all depend on whether your ex-husband's pension is higher or lower than the basic state pension to which you are entitled.

In addition, you would be entitled to any SERPS pension your husband had earned, as long as his SERPS pension combined with yours did not exceed the maximum SERPS pension for any one person. If your husband dies after 5 April 2000, you will only receive half his SERPS pension. Widows younger than their state pension age are also usually entitled to a £1,000 tax-free lump sum.

Widows aged under 45 at bereavement
Apart from the usual entitlement to a tax-free £1,000 lump sum, younger widows may have other entitlements:

○ A childless widow aged under 45 when her husband dies is not entitled to a widow's pension.

○ A widow under 45 with children will qualify for a single parent allowance.

○ A widow aged between 45 and 54 receives a pension based on her late husband's basic and SERPS pensions. This would be scaled down if he died when she was under 50. This is payable up to her normal state retirement age.

Action plan

○ If you are concerned about the pensions you are accumulating in any state schemes, use form BR19 (available from your local DSS or Benefits Agency office) to obtain a forecast of the pensions you could expect from the State. Remember that this is only a forecast.

○ If your state pension is likely to be lower than the maximum because of an interrupted National Insurance contributions history, you can choose to pay voluntary National Insurance contributions. See Chapter 13 for more details.

○ If you are currently contracted out of SERPS, using a personal pension, you should consider whether this is your best approach. Consult a qualified independent financial adviser.

5 Introduction to employers schemes

One of the biggest advantages of employers pension schemes compared with taking out a personal pension is that the employer will bear a significant part of the cost – usually a larger proportion than the employee.

Independent financial adviser and *Moneywise* Ask the Professionals panellist Keith Sanham says:

"A pension is a deferred salary. If you can't see why you should join your employer's pension scheme think of your employer's contribution as a pay rise now but receivable in the future."

Some schemes are non-contributory, meaning that the employer bears all of the cost of funding your pension. Some employers will pay into an employee's personal pension, but this is still unusual, especially if your employer already runs its own scheme.

Because your employer will pay such a large proportion of your pension, joining your company scheme is often your best option. But remember that this will always depend on individual circumstances.

The way schemes work differs from one company to another, and if you are a member of a company scheme already, or are thinking of joining one, you will find most of the information you need to know in the scheme booklet issued by your company scheme.

Almost all employers pension schemes have been approved by the Inland Revenue. They benefit from special treatment, and are known as 'exempt approved' pension schemes.

No other investment enjoys the same tax concessions as pension schemes:

○ All contributions – both yours and your employer's – benefit from tax relief. Your contributions enjoy relief at your highest rate. In most cases, contributions are deducted from your pre-tax earnings under the PAYE system.

○ The pension fund itself grows partly free of tax. Income from some investments is free of tax, as are any capital gains.

However, the second tax concession is now of limited benefit. When UK shares pay dividends they do so net of tax. Until July 1997 the funds could reclaim this tax, but this right was abolished in the 1997 Budget. This has made a difference to the attraction of pensions, but Chancellor Gordon Brown argues that many pensions have large surpluses, which means they can afford to lose this tax break (see page 67).

> Exempt approved pension schemes are allowed generous tax concessions by the Inland Revenue. Because these concessions mean less tax for the government's coffers, the Inland Revenue places restrictions on the amounts that can be put into these schemes, and the amount which can be taken out when you retire.

Most people in employers pension schemes are members of schemes which pay a pension based on their final salary at or near retirement. This type of scheme is known as a final salary scheme. It is sometimes also known as a 'defined benefit' scheme, because the amount of the pension payable is known in advance. Final salary schemes are covered in detail in Chapter 6.

The other common type of employers scheme is known as a 'money purchase' employers scheme. The amount you contribute is known from the outset, but the actual pension you receive depends on the investment gains from the fund invested on your behalf. This type of scheme is also known as a 'defined contribution' scheme. Money purchase schemes are covered in Chapter 7. The rest of this chapter explains features common to both types. Your employers pension department will be able to tell you which type of scheme is on offer.

Prior to 1988, your employer could have insisted that you joined the company's scheme. This has now changed, and you can choose not to join your company's scheme.

If you choose not to join your company scheme, your employer has to consider how to treat you. By not joining you may make yourself ineligible for any death in service benefit, or for early retirement on the grounds of ill health. Some companies provide part or all of these benefits, and others do not. Your company may offer you chances to join the scheme at a later date, or it may not.

Why should you join your employers pension scheme?

○ The best reason – almost without exception – for joining a company scheme is because the employer contributes to your pension. In fact your employer will usually make around two-thirds of the contributions to your pension.

○ If you choose to pay into a personal pension instead, it is unlikely that your employer will contribute – although some do.

○ If you expect to move jobs regularly, or plan to become self-employed in the near future, then you could con-sider paying into a personal pension scheme instead. But even so, if you think you will be with your current company for a few years, you would be unwise to miss out on the contri-butions from your employer by not joining the company scheme.

○ Of course, whether or not to join an employers pension scheme depends on your individual circum-stances. There are big pluses for joining, but if you have any doubts about the best course of action, you should consult an independent finan-cial adviser.

Inland Revenue rules

The Inland Revenue has set out the maximum benefits from occupa-tional schemes, and other conditions which must be met for a scheme to benefit from the generous tax concessions available.

Usually in this book the current rules for post-89 members will be taken to be the norm, and where the rules are different for pre-87 and 87/89 members, this will be indicated.

It is important to note that these constraints differ according to when you joined an employers pension scheme. There are three categories, and it is important to know which one you fall into:

○ Pre-87 members: This covers employees who were members of their company's scheme before 17 March 1987.

○ 87/89 members: This category includes employees who joined their company scheme between 17 March 1987 and 1 June 1989, but only if the scheme itself had been set up before 14 March 1989.

○ Post-89 members: You fall into this category if your scheme was set up on or after 14 March 1989, or if you joined a scheme established before that date and your date of joining was on or after 1 June 1989.

Although it is confusing to have these three categories, your pension is treated differently depending which one you come into – with significant differences in the size of pension you could expect to receive.

RETIREMENT AGE

A pension scheme can specify a normal retirement age anywhere between 60 and 75. Ages outside that range can be set only at the discretion of the Inland Revenue – for example if it is customary in that particular line of employment.

Following rulings by the European Court of Justice, employers pension schemes have to offer equal treatment between the sexes – including retirement ages. This means that most schemes have now equalised their pension ages for men and women, at an age of the scheme's choosing. This has more often resulted in women having to work until the retirement age previously specified for men, rather than the other way round. For example, although pre-87 and 87/89 schemes could be set up originally to allow women to retire at 55, this is no longer possible – they must now wait until 60, the minimum age allowed for men under those schemes.

> There are different retirement age ranges for pre-87 members and 87/89 members: they are 60 to 70 for men and 55 to 70 for women.

The Inland Revenue rules for employers schemes allow for early retirement from the age of 50. This has different implications for the different types of scheme – see page 81 for final salary schemes and page 93 for money purchase schemes.

The Inland Revenue also has rules for people who want to retire later than the normal retirement age specified in their company scheme. Your pension can continue to accrue benefits – in fact, if you have already reached the legal maximum of a pension equivalent to two-thirds final salary, in case of late retirement you can exceed this – but only up to a maximum of three-quarters final salary. The tax-free lump sum can

> If you know that you cannot complete 40 years of service and achieve the two-thirds pension, you have ways of boosting your pension. Your scheme may allow accelerated accrual (see page 62). Alternatively, you can top-up your pension (see Chapter 14).

Years of pensionable service at normal retirement age	Maximum pension as a proportion of final salary
1 to 5	1/60 for each year
6	8/60
7	16/60
8	24/60
9	32/60
10 or more	40/60

Example
You retired in 1990 at normal retirement age after seven years in a company. You joined the scheme in 1983, and are therefore a pre-87 member. Your salary at retirement was £30,000. Your scheme allowed the uplifted 60th scale to be used in calculating pension entitlement. After seven years, the maximum pension you would be allowed under this method would be 16/60 of your final salary – a maximum permitted pension of £8,000. Under the normal 1/60 rate of accrual, your maximum pension would have been 7/60 of £30,000 – a maximum permitted pension of only £3,500.

also accumulate above the normal limits – to a maximum 135/80 of final salary.

MAXIMUM PENSION

The Inland Revenue limits the pension payable at normal retirement age to no more than two-thirds of 'final salary'; confusingly this applies to both final salary and money purchase pensions. The usual way in which this entitlement is built up is by allowing a pension benefit of 1/60 of final salary for each year of pensionable service, up to a maximum of 40 years.

This means that if you retire from your job after 40 years pensionable service, the Inland Revenue's rules say that you can take a pension of 40/60 of your final salary. If you only have 30 years of service, then your maximum permitted pension is limited to 30/60 of your final salary. This calculation applies to all types of exempt approved schemes, whether they are money purchase schemes or final salary schemes.

So if your pension accrues at the rate of 1/60 for each year of service, you will have to be a member of the pension scheme for 40 years to obtain the maximum benefits. Very few people will do this. The Inland Revenue allows faster accrual rates, subject to the maximum limits it has set. These limits depend on the membership type. For pre-87 members, the two-thirds maximum pension can be permitted if the employee has completed ten years' service at normal retirement age. This is called the 'uplifted 60th scale'. Pension entitlement builds up as shown in the table on page 61.

For 87/89 and post-89 members, the Inland Revenue allows an accelerated accrual at the flat rate of 1/30 for each year of membership, until the maximum pension is reached at 20 years. This accelerated scale gives equal weight to each year of service – it does not weight the later years as the uplifted 60th scale does.

Remember that these accelerated rates are the Inland Revenue maximums. Whether it is possible for you to take advantage of them depends on the rules of your pension scheme; consult your handbook or speak to your pensions administrator.

Where accelerated accrual is used, the pension scheme has to take into account any other pension benefits you have accumulated – from previous employment, AVCs or personal pensions for example – to make sure that you do not exceed the limit.

Before we define what 'final salary' means, a brief word about the 'earnings cap', as introduced in the 1989 Finance Act.

The earnings cap limits the size of the final salary on which you can base your pension. Currently, in 1998/99, the earnings cap is set at £87,600. This means that you cannot take any salary over and above £87,600 into account when calculation your pension. If you earn £100,000, your maximum final

> Your employer by law has to provide you with a form P11D by 6 July each year. This specifies the benefits on which you have to pay Schedule E tax, and the taxable value specified for each benefit.

> **Example**
> An 87/89 or post-89 member retiring on a salary of £30,000 from a scheme which allows accrual under the accelerated scale would have a maximum permitted entitlement of 7/30 – double the entitlement if the scheme only allowed 1/60 accrual. The maximum permitted pension in this example would be £7,000.

> **Example**
> You calculate your final salary using Method 1 (see page 64), and arrive at a figure of £110,000. Under the rules, you must repeat the calculation, this time using Method 2.
> Method 2 gives you a result of £95,000. Under the rules, you use £100,000 as your final salary – not the actual figure calculated.

Independent financial adviser and *Moneywise* Ask the Professionals panellist Kean Seager says:

"If you are currently a pre-87 or 87/89 member of a pension scheme you are in a privileged position. Be wary of leaving the scheme – if you do and join another you will automatically become subject to the earnings cap in the new scheme, whether it is an employers pension or a personal pension."

Example
You are a pre-87 member of your employers scheme earning £87,000 a year: assuming that you retire on the full two-thirds pension, your pension will be £58,000.

You plan to move to a new company and join its scheme. Your salary will be £90,000. Joining the company's scheme makes you a post-89 member, and the earnings cap comes into effect. You can only take the first £84,000 of your salary into account when planning your pension so your maximum pension would be limited to two-thirds of £84,000, or £56,000 – your salary will be higher but your pension lower.

salary is still £87,600 for the purpose of your pension – and the maximum allowable pension is £58,400, two-thirds of that amount.

The important thing to remember about the earnings cap is that it only applies to Post-89 members. So if you fall into one of the other categories described previously, the earnings cap does not apply to you. Pre-87 and 87/89 members can still take their full final salaries into account when planning their pensions.

Although for most people the earnings cap seems sufficiently high for them not to worry about it at the moment, in the future this may change:

○ The earnings cap has been increased most years since it was introduced. The Chancellor of the Exchequer did not increase it in the 1993/94 tax year – and that could happen again.
○ On top of that, the earnings cap, when it is increased, is increased in line with the RPI. The RPI usually moves more slowly than the increase in national average earnings, so the real value of the earnings cap is decreasing all the time. Eventually, most people can expect to be caught by it, especially if you have a number of years to go before you retire.

If you think that you will be caught by the earnings cap, then you must expect that not all of your income will be taken into account when calculating your pension from your company scheme. In this situation you should consider other forms of saving for retirement to make up this shortfall (see Chapter 13).

The Inland Revenue's definition of final salary specifies that it is the remuneration on which you have been liable for tax under Schedule E (under the rules for those who pay tax through the PAYE system). This definition includes not just your basic salary, but also any overtime, bonuses or perks on which you have paid Schedule E tax. So if you have a company car, the taxable value of that car can be included as part of your final salary.

The Inland Revenue also allows two different methods of calculating maximum final salary. It is the greater of:

Method 1: The remuneration on which you have been liable for Schedule E tax for any one of the five years before normal retirement age. For the year chosen, you take the basic earnings in that year. To that you add the average of all fluctuating payments – bonuses, overtime, commissions and taxable benefits – over at least three consecutive years ending in the year chosen.

Method 2: The annual average of total remuneration – basic earnings plus bonuses, overtime, etc. – on which you have been liable for Schedule E tax over three or more consecutive years ending in the last ten years before retirement.

If you are a controlling director (see page 101), you have to use method 2. If you are a pre-87 or 87/89 member, then if method 1 produces a final salary greater than £100,000, you have to use method 2. If method 2 produces a figure greater than £100,000, then the method 2 figure is used. If method 2 produces a figure less than £100,000, then £100,000 is used as the final salary.

Most companies use the first version when calculating your final remuneration (this will be specified in your pension scheme handbook), but it is worth remembering that the other method exists. For example, if your salary in your final years of work is lower than in earlier years (perhaps because you have been winding down in anticipation of your retirement), then method 2 will produce a bigger final remuneration. It will not change the pension you are entitled to under your company scheme, but it could allow you to plan to boost your pension through top-ups (see Chapter 14).

Tax expert and *Moneywise* Ask the Professionals panellist Janet Adam says:

"Employees should check the rules of their scheme carefully. There is no requirement for companies to pay the maximum pension allowed by the Inland Revenue, even with a final salary scheme."

MAXIMUM CONTRIBUTIONS

You are not allowed to contribute more than 15% of your salary to your company scheme. Like final salary, your salary for the purpose of pension contributions is your basic salary plus bonuses, overtime, and any other taxable benefits you may receive, such as a company car or private health insurance cover. Where the earnings cap applies – to post-89 members – you can contribute a maximum of 15% of your salary up to the earnings cap of £87,600 (1998/99). There is no limit set by the Inland Revenue on how much your employer is allowed to contribute to your pension.

Employers' contributions

Putting it simply, the employer contributes as much as is necessary to make sure that the scheme will meet its liabilities; this is obviously most important with a final salary scheme. In practice, of course, the process is more complicated than that, but the basic principle is the same.

Pension schemes are required to appoint an actuary, and one of the actuary's responsibilities is to produce a valuation report on the scheme every three years. As a part of this valuation report, the actuary will propose a level at which the employer's contributions are set, in order that the scheme can meet its liabilities. The actuary's aim is to set a contribution rate which is stable, but which will make sure that the scheme is properly funded over the longer term.

To do this, the actuary must take into account the membership mix of the scheme – life expectancy, for example, will differ from scheme to scheme according to the ages of the members and the mix between the sexes. The number of married members and their children will also affect the scheme's future liabilities. The actuary also has to take into account reasonable assumptions about the profits which could be expected from the various types of investments, and also the likely future salary increases on which pensions will be based.

These assumptions can be knocked off course by factors outside the control either of the actuary or the pension scheme itself. For example, a stockmarket crash, or a return to high levels of inflation, will seriously affect the assumptions made when an actuary carried out a pension fund valuation. Actuaries, who are by profession cautious people, build a degree of protection into their assumptions because of factors like this.

How much can you contribute to your employers pension scheme?

Use this calculator to work out the maximum contributions you can make to your pension:

£

Annual salary (gross basic from payslip)

Annual bonuses, overtime

Profit related pay (gross)

Taxable value (from your P11D) of:

Company car

Private health cover

Mobile phone

Other benefits

TOTAL EARNINGS

Does the earnings cap apply?   Yes/No

If Yes and your total earnings are more than £87,600, write £87,600 in Revised Total Earnings below

If No, write your total earnings in Revised Total Earnings below

REVISED TOTAL EARNINGS

Maximum pension contribution
Revised Total Earnings x 15%

It is usually easier to set a stable contributions rate from the employer when the scheme is a large one. Relatively simple things – unusually large pay rises, or the retirement of senior staff – can affect the liabilities of a small scheme considerably.

The actuary's aim is, of course, to make sure that the scheme is 100% funded. Because the actuary will always build in an element of caution when calculating the employer's contribution level, the scheme may become overfunded – its assets become greater than the liabilities it needs to cover. In addition, better investment performance may occur than that forecast, also taking the scheme into surplus.

Where a large surplus exists, an employer may want to take that money out of the pension fund and put it back into the business. Generally, if this happens, the employer will be expected to use the surplus first to make improvements to pensions being paid out to existing pensioners, and also improve the benefits to current members. Any surplus left after that may be taken by the employer. If this happens, the Inland Revenue will tax that surplus – on the grounds that up to this point both the pension contributions and the investment gains have been largely tax free.

An alternative course of action when a pension scheme is overfunded is for the employer to take a 'contributions holiday'; with the agreement of the trustees and the actuary, the employer will stop making contributions for a specified period until the surplus in the fund reduces.

The Pensions Act 1995 introduced a new requirement of 'adequate funding', which adds a further protection to members of final salary pension schemes (see page 76).

Employers scheme benefits

These include lump sums, death in service payouts and pensions, and pensions for dependants who outlive you.

LUMP SUMS

The Inland Revenue allows you to take part of your pension entitlement as a tax-free lump sum. If you take this option, the lump sum comes out of the fund you have built up to pay for your pension, so the actual pension you receive will be smaller if you take a lump sum. Check first that your company scheme will let you take a lump sum: although most schemes allow this, they are not obliged to do so. The lump sum is tax free, and is limited by the Inland Revenue to no more than 1·5 times your final salary. Therefore, if your final salary is £50,000, the maximum lump sum you could take would be £75,000.

Years of pensionable service at normal retirement age	Maximum lump sum as a proportion of final salary
1 to 8	3/80 for each year
9	30/80
10	36/80
11	42/80
12	48/80
13	54/80
14	63/80
15	72/80
16	81/80
17	90/80
18	99/80
19	108/80
20 or more	120/80

You are not automatically entitled to this lump sum, and the maximum amount depends on length of service in the scheme, and the size of the pension you have built up. Entitlement to the lump sum normally accrues at a rate of 3/80 of final salary for each year of pensionable service, up to 40 years. After 40 years you are entitled to a lump sum of 120/80 (1·5 times) final salary.

Again, the Inland Revenue will allow this entitlement to build up faster than the 3/80 rate. Whether you can take advantage of this accelerated rate depends on the rules of your pension scheme. The Inland Revenue's regulations differ according to membership type.

Pre-87 members
This category is allowed to take the full 1·5 times final salary lump sum after 20 years, on an uplifted 80th scale (see table above).

87/89 members
This category accrues the entitlement to the lump sum on the normal 3/80

scale. If the 87/89 member's pension scheme accrues pension benefit faster than the 1/60 rate, an enhanced lump sum may be allowed. The calculation to do this is complicated – if your pension scheme allows this method to be used, consult your scheme administrator.

Post-89 members
The maximum lump sum entitlement is the greater of:

○ 1·5 times final salary.
○ Or 2·25 times the actual pension the member could take, before any of the pension is surrendered to pay for the lump sum itself, or any survivor pensions.

Remember that there can be limits on the size of final salary (which hence will limit the size of the lump sum):

○ Pre-87 and 87/89 members may be limited by the '£100,000 rule' (see page 62).
○ Post-89 members are limited by the earnings cap (£87,600 in 1998/99).

It should also be noted that in the case of contracted out pension schemes, no tax-free lump sum can be taken from the SERPS-related pension.

MAXIMUM SURVIVOR PENSIONS

If you die in retirement, your pension scheme will probably pay a pension for your surviving spouse/partner and/or dependent children:

○ For a pension scheme which is contracted out of SERPS, the Inland Revenue requires that it must pay a survivor pension equivalent to 50% of the SERPS-related pension.
○ For the remainder of the pension, the Inland Revenue has set no legal requirement to pay survivor pensions – it depends on the way your pension scheme was set up. However, the Inland Revenue has set limits on any survivor pensions which may be paid, as follows:
  • a spouse's pension may not be more than two-thirds of the pension the member was entitled to;
  • pensions may be paid to dependent children as well as (or instead of) the spouse. The total pensions paid may not exceed the pension to which the member was entitled, and no one person can receive more

than two-thirds of the total pension paid to all the survivors.

A dependent child is considered to be one aged under 18, or if aged over 18, still in full-time education.

The Inland Revenue has become more flexible in its attitude in recent years about the payment of a survivor pension to an adult to whom you are not married. It will allow schemes to pay pensions to such adults who have been financially dependent on the pension scheme member, for example where the two adults have depended on both their incomes to support their lifestyle.

DEATH IN SERVICE BENEFITS

Consider these statistics: 24% of men aged 18 will die before they reach 65, and 9% of women aged 18 will die before they reach 60.

If you are contributing to a pension scheme and die before retirement age, then in theory your pension contributions could be completely wasted – and your dependants could receive nothing. Fortunately, almost all pension schemes provide death in service benefits, even though the government requirement is only that they provide a survivor pension from the SERPS-related portion. However, where pension schemes offer death in service benefits, the Inland Revenue sets maximum limits on what can be paid to the beneficiaries.

Life insurance
The scheme can pay a lump sum life insurance benefit of up to four times the member's annual salary. This is subject to the earnings cap (see page 69). If you are a pre-87 or 87/89 member, the earnings cap does not apply.

How much – if anything – is actually paid depends on your pension scheme, as does the definition of annual salary. Consult your pension scheme booklet or scheme administrator for details.

This lump sum is not subject to income tax, and the pension scheme is usually set up to make the payment at the discretion of the pension scheme trustees. This is to make sure that there is no inheritance tax liability on the payment.

Refund of contributions
The scheme can refund contributions paid by the member. Tax at the rate of 20% will be deducted.

Survivor Pensions

The limits on survivor pensions are the same as those which apply to death in retirement (see page 69):

○ A spouse's pension may not be more than two-thirds of the pension the member was entitled to.
○ Pensions may be paid to dependent children as well as (or instead of) the spouse. The total pensions paid may not exceed the pension to which the member was entitled, and no one person can receive more than two-thirds of the total pension paid to the dependants.

The scheme must use the SERPS-related element of the pension to pay a survivor pension, which must be 50% of the member's pension from that SERPS-related element.

How employers pensions are run

Before the Inland Revenue will consider a scheme as an 'exempt approved' scheme and grant it the tax concessions outlined on page 57, it must be set up under a trust.

When a pension scheme is set up, a trust deed is drawn up which is legally binding and which outlines the powers of the trustees. Basically these are as follows:

○ The power to hold the assets of the scheme – subject to the powers outlined in the trust deed or in the scheme rules – and to use those assets to benefit the scheme and its members.
○ The power to determine all questions arising from the scheme, so the trustees are the final point of reference should there be any query about the way the scheme ought to work.
○ The power to carry out any transaction in connection with the scheme.

A company which runs a pension scheme will usually appoint most of the trustees, although the 1995 Pensions Act specifies that there should also be trustees nominated by the members of the scheme. Unfortunately, there are ways in which a company can get round this requirement,

How do you become a trustee?

If you want to become a trustee of your pension scheme, find out from your pensions administrator what the company's policy is. Most companies will appoint member-nominated trustees as required under the 1995 Pensions Act. If this is the case with your scheme, then you will probably have to stand for election as a trustee at the next opportunity. Other schemes may simply appoint a certain number of trustees who are ordinary members of the scheme, without having them nominated or elected by the members. In this case, if you indicate to your employer that you are willing to be considered as a trustee, they will take you into consideration when a vacancy occurs.

If you do decide to become a trustee, you must remember that it is a role which carries particular responsibilities, even though the workload may not be heavy. You should be prepared to remain a trustee for a number of years, and take the trouble to understand the scheme and how it works. The reward is that you can play a part in improving the scheme for the benefit of all its members.

There are other people involved in running a pension whom you may encounter as a trustee:

○ **Pension managers**
Managers can be appointed to run the administration of the scheme, but the trustees retain responsibility.

○ **Actuaries**
Actuaries are trained in mathematics and the science of risk in order to be able to work out the balance between the assets held by the scheme and the liabilities it can expect to have to pay out. They are also responsible for ensuring that a pension fund is solvent and run properly.

Actuaries have to ensure there are enough funds available to meet all current liabilities, and that there is the right mix of investments to ensure stability and growth to meet all future liabilities. They also have a duty to be whistle-blowers if they suspect that any wrongdoing is taking place.

○ **Fund managers**
The fund managers will probably be external specialists who manage money on behalf of a selection of pension funds. It is a very competitive business and pension funds can switch managers if the fund manager's performance is not up to scratch. A new manager will be chosen after a 'beauty parade' of competing fund managers has taken place.

○ **Pensions consultancy firms**
These firms are able to advise on the overall structure and planning of a pension fund, and can offer advice to trustees to help them to fulfil all their duties.

A trust is an arrangement under which property – in this case the assets of the pension scheme – is held by one person or a group of people – the trustees – for the benefit of another group of people. The trustees are not able to benefit themselves from the property which has been entrusted to them, except that the trustees are also allowed to be members of the pension scheme.

though a reputable organisation should have no desire to do so; the more open the scheme is to its members, the better for all concerned.

To be a trustee, you need to have the legal capacity to hold property, so, for example, those under 18 or certified as insane cannot be trustees.

By setting up a trust, the employer has created a legal separation between the money intended for pension provision, and the normal trading income and expenses of the business. The employer cannot legally use the money in the pension fund in order to bail out a struggling business. There are famous examples of employers who have appropriated pension funds illegally but after the 1995 Pensions Act, this should be much harder to do.

The employer cannot tell the trustees what to do with the assets of the scheme, but if all the trustees are appointed by the employer, there is a danger that they will allow themselves to be influenced. Again, if the scheme has member-nominated trustees, there will be more protection of assets intended for the members.

Trustees are therefore in a position of great responsibility; they have to set out the principles of investment of the scheme, so that it can benefit from the best financial returns with the least risk to the fund. They have to ensure that the scheme is operated in the best interests of its members, and they must act impartially at all times, and must therefore separate their trustee activities entirely from the role they would normally perform in the company. They must ensure that they are acting within the provisions of the trust deed, and they must make sure that they know the scheme inside out.

INVESTMENT

Contributions to employers pensions are made by employers and employees into a pooled fund. This fund is then invested according to guidelines drawn up by the trustees of the scheme. These guidelines specify which types of investment are allowed for the pension fund.

Some types of investment may be ruled out because the trustees consider them too risky, for example shares in companies in the developing world. Or trustees may exclude categories of investment on ethical grounds, for example shares in tobacco companies and the armaments industry.

The trustees will also specify the allowed overall mix of investment, limiting certain categories to no more than a certain percentage of the total. For example, they may specify that shares in Far East companies make up no more than 5% of the total investment. This is to ensure that the spread of investments is wide enough to avoid serious losses if a particular investment sector, such as property, performs badly compared with other investments. Many pension scheme trustees now avoid investing in UK property following the prolonged slump in property values and the reverses suffered by some pension funds during the late 1980s.

The aim of the pension fund trustees is to maximise gains for the pension fund through a sensible investment policy, at an acceptable level of risk to the pension fund itself. Any restrictions on the trustees' own freedom to dictate the investment policy will have been set out in the trust document.

Trustees usually appoint professional fund managers to invest the assets of the pension scheme. It is possible to have in-house fund managers, but few companies bother to do this nowadays, as using professional fund managers lessens the cost and allows access to a wider range of fund management experience.

The nature of the investment programme will also differ according to the membership of the scheme. Where the membership is young – in a new scheme set up by a new company, for example – the pension fund can afford to invest more heavily in shares, where the risk of short-term losses may be greater (especially in overseas shares), but the potential for long-term gains is very high. Since the membership is young, the liabilities of the scheme are small in the short term –

after all, it will be perhaps 20 or 30 years before it will have to pay pensions for most of its members – and it can afford to invest for long-term gains.

Where the membership of a scheme is more mature, and a high proportion of members is either already retired or approaching retirement, the scheme is less able to risk short-term losses. The trustees will then concentrate their investment policy on less risky investments such as gilts, which promise a fixed-interest return on the capital invested.

It is quite common for trustees to appoint two firms of fund managers, either to handle separate parts of the investment – for example, one firm may be a specialist in a particular field – or in order to encourage competition between the two fund managers; the harder the fund managers work, the better the outcome should be for the pension fund.

Employers pension schemes are measured by external specialists. This allows the trustees to measure the performance of their fund managers –and hence of the fund itself – against the pension funds of other companies. The fund managers are often set performance targets in relation to these external measurements; for example, they may be asked to produce investment returns which are above the average of all the pension schemes analysed in the survey to which your scheme subscribes.

The majority of pension schemes manage their investments in the manner described above. Smaller schemes often operate with more simple methods of providing the pension fund necessary to meet its liabilities:

○ The scheme can use an insurance company, paying over the contributions from members and from the employer in order effectively to buy an insurance policy which will pay out the necessary benefits.
○ Instead of managing their spread of investments themselves, schemes can participate in funds managed by an insurance company or specialist investment company. These managed funds work in a similar way to unit trusts. Participants purchase units in a collective fund which is run by a fund manager. This fund will be invested in a spread of investments. For smaller schemes, participating in this type of pooled investment will bring economies of scale. The range of investments will also be wider than a small scheme could invest in safely and economically.

Independent financial adviser and *Moneywise* Ask the Professionals panellist Keith Sanham says:

"Raiding a pension scheme is no different to mugging old age pensioners. Who would do such a thing?"

PROTECTION

Although the trustees of a pension scheme are responsible for ensuring that the scheme is not mismanaged – or worse, raided by an unscrupulous employer – the discovery that Robert Maxwell had stolen £400m from the Mirror Group pension scheme highlighted that there were failings in the system. As a result of that scandal, and others, the government passed the 1995 Pensions Act, which aims to improve the protection of pension schemes. Most of the provisions in the Act came into effect in April 1997.

The Act sets up a new regulator, the Occupational Pensions Regulatory Authority (OPRA), with powers to investigate schemes if something appears to be going wrong. It will depend on being informed of irregularities by trustees, actuaries, auditors and employees. They will act as 'whistle-blowers' when they identify something improper taking place with regard to a pension scheme's assets.

As discussed above, the 1995 Pensions Act creates member-nominated trustees. Unless the scheme adopts a procedure to avoid appointing member-nominated trustees, those trustees must be allocated one-third of the trustee appointments. The Act requires that final salary schemes be adequately funded. This means that if the scheme were to shut down, it should have funds sufficient to meet all its liabilities, being able to pay transfer values for all non-retired members, and buy annuities to pay the pensions of all retired members. This requirement takes effect in 2002. After that date, if a final salary scheme is not adequately funded, the trustees and the employer have to agree a plan which requires the employer to restore adequate funding within five years.

Exceptionally, if the funding of a final salary scheme falls below 90% of the adequate funding level, the employer has to put enough extra funding into the scheme within the next 12 months to restore it to 90% funding. After that, of course, it would have to move on to the five-year plan to bring the funding up to 100%.

The other aspect of investor protection in the 1995 Pensions Act is the introduction of a compensation scheme which will pay out where a scheme has lost assets through fraud, dishonesty or intentional misappropriation of the assets, and where the company has become insolvent.

Apart from the above measures designed for investor protection, there were a number of other changes introduced in the 1995 Pensions Act. Most are discussed elsewhere in this book, but briefly, they are:

○ Changes to the requirements concerning the SERPS-related pension in a contracted-out scheme.

○ Employers schemes will have to have internal grievance procedures as a first resort for members.

○ The non-SERPS part of final salary scheme pensions must increase in line with RPI or 5% (if lower; see page 52).

○ The National Insurance contribution rebates for contracting out become age related for money purchase occupational pension schemes and personal pension schemes (see Chapters 7 and 10).

○ Personal pension holders can defer buying an annuity when they retire, and can draw income from the pension fund instead. They can defer purchasing an annuity until age 75 (See Chapters 10 and 16).

○ Courts now have the power to allocate part of a husband's or wife's pension to the other party in the case of a divorce (see page 35).

○ The state pension age has been equalised at 65 for men and for women born after April 1955. Women born before April 1950 still retire at 60; women born between those two dates retire according to an age-related scale (see Chapter 4).

○ Employers pension schemes must treat men and women equally. This provision came into effect from 1 January 1996.

Eligibility for membership

This will be laid out in the scheme rules. There will be a minimum age for joining, and often you are required to have worked for the company for a period of time – say six months – before you will be invited to join the scheme.

The scheme decides which categories of its workforce are eligible to join it, and it does not have to be open to everyone. For example, many schemes restrict membership to full-time permanent employees, excluding part-timers and temporary or casual workers. Schemes do have to be careful with restrictions of this nature, in case they fall foul of employment law. For example, since part-timers are very often women, excluding this category could be considered as sex discrimination. Excluding women directly, or admitting them under different conditions, has been illegal under UK law since 1978. And indirect discrimination, such as excluding groups of workers who are more likely to be women, is also illegal, following rulings at the European Court of Justice.

All employers schemes have three categories of members:

○ Current employees of the company, who are members of the pension scheme and who are contributing to that scheme.
○ Employees who have left the company but who are not taking their pension. Typically these will be people who have left to go to another job, or people who have been made redundant. The pension rights they have accumulated are still held within the scheme; this is called a preserved pension.
○ People who are receiving their pensions. They may have retired at the normal age, or taken early retirement, perhaps because of ill health.

People who leave their employer and join a new employer have the option of having their pension rights transferred to the new employer. Once this transfer has been made, they no longer have any connection with their old pension scheme. See Chapter 9 for more details.

YOUR PENSION SCHEME BOOKLET

Much of the important information you need to know about your employer's scheme can be found in the pension scheme booklet which your company scheme has to publish. Get a copy from your pensions administrator and read it carefully; it should cover the following points:

○ The normal retirement age in your pension scheme.
○ The rate at which your pension will accumulate.
○ What the maximum lump sum will be.
○ What your contributions to the scheme are.
○ Death in service benefits such as life insurance and survivor pensions.
○ Survivor pensions in the case of death after retirement.

If you do not understand any of the points in the handbook, ask to meet your pensions administrator and get him or her to discuss them with you.

You have the right to a free copy of the scheme handbook while you are considering whether or not to join.

Action plan

○ If you are not in your company scheme, and are eligible to join it, you should think very carefully about joining. This kind of scheme is the best option in most circumstances.

○ Make sure that you are fully aware of how your scheme works – how it defines final salary, whether you can take a lump sum, retirement date, etc. Get a copy of your scheme handbook and study it. If you do not understand any of the points in the the handbook, contact your scheme's administrator.

○ Make sure that your instructions are up to date concerning the beneficiaries of your death in service benefits. Likewise make sure that you have planned for survivor pensions for your spouse or partner and for any dependent children.

○ Consider becoming a trustee of the scheme, so that you can have a say in how it is run.

6 Final salary employers schemes

Most employers schemes pay a pension based on their members' final salary at or near retirement. This is known as a final salary or defined benefit scheme, because the amount of the pension payable is known in advance.

How final salary is calculated

It is important to make sure that you know your company scheme's definition of 'final salary' as it can make a major difference to the actual pension you will be paid under the company scheme.

The Inland Revenue's definition is on page 62, but your employer can choose to ignore some elements which the Inland Revenue would allow. It is vital to check all these facts. If your scheme makes exclusions along the lines of those listed below – and lots do – your final pension will be less

---

Check in your employers scheme handbook to see how final salary has been defined:

○ Does it include bonuses and overtime, or exclude them?

○ If you are entitled to profit-related pay, will this be considered part of your final salary?

○ Will taxable benefits such as a company car or private medical insurance be included in the calculation? The Inland Revenue places a value on these benefits for taxation purposes, and it allows this value to be taken into account when calculating final pay.

○ Does your company scheme include all of your basic salary, or will it exclude the first £3,000 or so of your salary on the grounds that the basic state pension will provide that retirement income?

Example

You are about to retire, and have been a member of the company scheme for 40 years. You have therefore built up the maximum entitlement of two-thirds final salary. On top of your basic salary you receive a bonus of up to 15% of your salary. Because the company is doing well, for most of the last few years you have received the full bonus and you have become used to that extra cash to support the lifestyle you want. You also have a company car, but when you retire you will have to buy your own car.

Your income (adjusted for inflation, and including the notional taxable value of the car) over the last three years has been:

Year	Basic salary	Bonus	Car (notional value)	Total
1996	27,000	4,050	2,800	33,850
1997	29,000	4,350	2,800	36,150
1998	30,000	4,500	2,800	37,300
Average of last three years	**28,667**	**4,300**	**2,800**	**35,767**

The maximum pension you can take is two-thirds final salary, but it all depends on how your scheme defines final salary. Look at the differences:

○ Under Inland Revenue rules you can include bonuses and perks such as your car. Basing your pension on an average of the last three years' salaries, under Inland Revenue rules your maximum pension can be two-thirds of £35,767 – your average total income including bonus and car. This would allow you a pension of £23,845.

○ Your scheme may not allow you to include your company car in the calculations. This would reduce your average final salary to £32,967 – and your pension to £21,978. If your scheme also excludes your bonus, then the calculation is made on the average of your last three years' basic salaries only. Your pension would then be two-thirds of £28,667, which is £19,111.

○ Finally, your scheme may exclude an amount of your salary equivalent to the basic state pension. For example, this might exclude the first £3,300 of your salary when your pension is calculated, reducing your pension to only two-thirds of £25,367, which is only £16,911.

In this example, the difference between the methods of defining final salary could produce an annual difference in pension of up to £6,934!

than you might have expected.

DEFINITION OF FINAL SALARY

If your scheme's definition of final salary is less than generous, there is little you can do to change the scheme. Improvements to the scheme may be planned for the future – ask the pensions administrator, or one of the trustees.

The main reason why it is important to know how final salary is defined from the outset is that your pension planning will be considerably affected by this basic information. For example, it will be an important factor when deciding whether or not to join your company scheme.

It will also be important in any decision you may take to top up your pension. If the pension you can expect on retirement is below the maximum allowed by the Inland Revenue there are steps you can take to boost that pension (see Chapter 14).

A final salary pension scheme works by promising a pension equivalent to a fraction of your final salary for each year of membership of the scheme.

The majority of final salary schemes adopt the following approach:

○ For each year of membership, you accrue 1/60 of your final salary as a pension.

○ The maximum number of years of service which can count towards your pension is 40.

○ Therefore, by the time you retire, it is possible for you to have accrued 40 years' service, at 1/60 of final salary for each year of service.

○ The maximum pension you could take at retirement is therefore 40/60 – or two-thirds – of final salary.

Not all pension schemes operate on a 1/60 basis; some are more favourable, offering a build-up rate of 1/50 or 1/45 a year. With these schemes you can reach the maximum two-thirds pension in less than 40 years. Other schemes operate on a less

Example
With this type of scheme you are entitled to 1/60 of your final salary for each year you work and are a member of your pension scheme. So after 15 years you will be entitled to 15/60 of your final salary as a pension; after 30 years, you will be entitled to 30/60; and after 40 years you will reach the full pension entitlement of 40/60 of final salary – the full two-thirds pension which is allowed by the Inland Revenue.

favourable basis. Public sector schemes accrue the pension on a 1/80 basis. There are, however, other features of a public sector scheme that make it an attractive proposition (see 'Public sector pension schemes' on page 85).

Your scheme handbook will specify the rules applying to your own company scheme for the way your pension builds up. As discussed, this will be on the basis that each year of service earns you a proportion of your final pension. There will be a maximum number of years needed to build up a pension of two-thirds final salary.

The Inland Revenue limits your pension to two-thirds final salary so, in the example earlier, if you worked 45 years you would not be allowed to build your pension beyond the 40/60 maximum – unless you are taking late retirement (see page 60). You should be aware of this problem if you are likely to have worked more than the maximum number of years required for full pension by the time you retire.

> Independent financial adviser and *Moneywise* Ask the Professionals panellist Brian Dennehy says:
>
> "More than nine out of ten people in company schemes retire on less than maximum benefits, and less than one in five make additional voluntary contributions. You must take action as early as possible to discover what your shortfall will be, and how you can fill this gap."

Check in the handbook or talk to your pension scheme administrator to find out what happens in this circumstance. Some pension schemes let you halt your contributions at this stage. Others require you to go on paying, even though it is not directly of benefit to you; the reason for this is that you are subsidising the pension contributions of other members – as other people may have done in the past for you. Over all, the scheme may argue that you have benefited in the past from this cross-subsidy by paying slightly lower contributions each month than you might have done otherwise.

Early retirement

If you have to retire because of ill health, the rules for a final salary scheme allow you to retire on the pension you would have received at your normal retirement age, calculated as a proportion of your current salary.

There must be 20 years between the date of your joining the scheme and the date when you would normally have retired, otherwise the benefits are reduced.

If you are medically certified as having a very short life expectancy you can exchange your entire pension entitlement for a cash lump sum. In this circumstance, part of the lump sum will be considered the equivalent of the one you could have taken in exchange for part of your pension (1·5 times your pensionable salary). This part will be tax free. Any lump sum cash in excess of the tax-free element will be taxed.

If you retire early for a reason other than ill health, the pension to which you are entitled is scaled down in proportion to your length of service.

Other types of final salary scheme

Teachers, members of the police force and NHS workers have the opportunity to join good final salary employers pension schemes.

Unfortunately, many of them were victims of the pensions mis-selling scandal of the late 1980s – they were persuaded to transfer from these schemes to a personal pension. As a result, many of them would lose out – see page 135 for more details of the compensation that may be available.

PUBLIC SECTOR PENSION SCHEMES
Around 4·5 million workers are members of public sector schemes. The schemes fall into two main types:

Public service schemes
These are set up by statutes, and include employees in central and local government, the police, the health service, teachers, the fire service and the armed forces. Predominantly they offer pension accrual on a 1/80 basis, but with a non-optional tax-free lump sum accruing at 3/80, which does not affect the pension entitlement. In contrast to this a private sector scheme may offer an optional lump sum, but taking the lump sum reduces the size of the pension payable. Therefore, a public service scheme offering 1/80 accrual and a non-optional lump sum can result in a very similar payout to a private sector scheme accruing on a 1/60 basis, with an

Example
Twins are retiring aged 65, and both are retiring on the maximum pension. Twin A is a member of a public service scheme accruing on a 1/80 basis, and Twin B is in a private sector scheme accruing on a 1/60 basis; both have a final salary of £30,000.

Twin A can take a pension of 40/80 of £30,000. That makes his pension £15,000. In addition, he will receive a lump sum of 1·5 times final salary – a tax-free lump sum of £45,000.

Twin B has two options:
○ He can take a salary of 40/60 of £30,000 and no lump sum: this would give him a pension of £20,000, but no lump sum.

○ He can take a lump sum of 1·5 times his final salary – a tax-free lump sum of £45,000. Doing so reduces his pension (at the rate of £1 a year for every £9 taken in the lump sum: £45,000/9 = £5,000) to £15,000.

So if he takes the lump sum, Twin B ends up with a retirement package identical to his brother's under the public service scheme.

optional lump sum.

Public service schemes also have other differences:

○ The pensions paid are linked to the full RPI.
○ They usually give better treatment in cases of early retirement.
○ Transfers between public service schemes benefit from membership of the 'Public Sector Transfer Club'. This results in better pension transfers between participating schemes than is often the case when the transfers are between private sector schemes.
○ These schemes need not necessarily be funded in the same way as private sector schemes. Some operate on a 'pay as you go' basis. There is no real risk of the scheme not paying out a pension, since they are established by statutes.

Public sector schemes
These schemes are established under trusts – like private sector schemes. They include employees in the nationalised industries, and are funded in the same way that private schemes are funded. For the most part, however, they still offer full RPI indexing of pensions, however, and they are members of the Public Sector Transfer Club.

Action plan

○ Check your scheme handbook to find out your scheme's exact definition of final salary.

○ What is the difference between the figure given and the Inland Revenue maximum?

○ Does your scheme exclude bonuses or other benefits?

○ Does it make a deduction for the basic state pension?

○ If so, then you have room to consider topping up your pension (for full details, see Chapter 14).

○ What is your scheme's retirement date? Is it the date that you would like to retire?

○ Does your scheme allow early retirement, and, if so, on what terms?

○ If they are not favourable, you should again look at ways of topping up your pension (see Chapter 14), or think about making other savings for your retirement. (see Chapter 15).

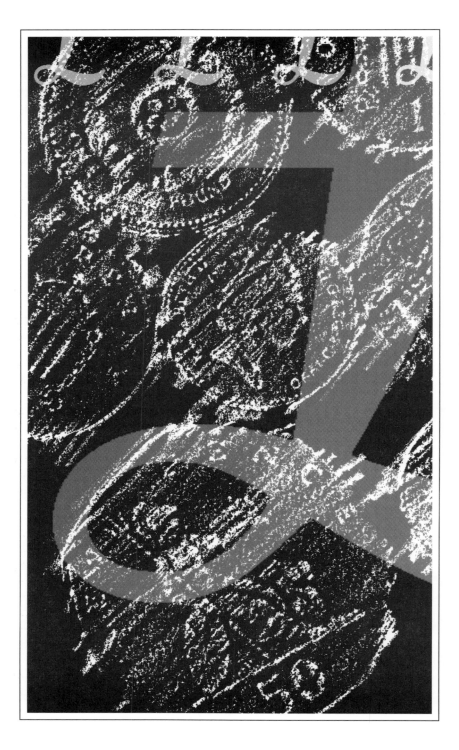

7 Money purchase employers schemes

Money purchase employers pension schemes operate under much the same regulatory regime as final salary employers schemes. However, the schemes themselves work in a very different way from final salary schemes.

This chapter should be read in conjunction with Chapter 5, which covers the topics common to employers pension schemes regardless of type, and which sets out the Inland Revenue limits.

With a money purchase scheme, the amount paid by the employee and employer is defined from the outset. This type of scheme is often also known as a defined contribution scheme. The size of the pension is not defined – this is the major difference from a final salary scheme, where you know from the outset how much your pension will be, but you and your employer do not know how much the total contributions will cost.

The size of the pension payable at retirement depends on the pension scheme assets relating to the individual member, although the pension paid cannot be more than the Inland Revenue limit of two-thirds final salary at normal retirement. Although the pension fund itself does not accrue on a 'years' basis (the way it would in a final salary scheme), but simply on the basis of the investment of the contributions made, the Inland Revenue entitlement to pension benefits still works on the basis of 'years'.

Your pension scheme has to state the basis on which the benefit accrues – commonly on a 60th basis, but the Inland Revenue allows faster rates of accrual (see Chapter 5). So if you have 30 years' service in such a scheme, you can take only a 30/60 – one-half – pension when you retire. This limit is then applied to the pension fund built up in your name, to make sure that it does not produce a pension greater than that limit.

Money purchase schemes are often found in companies where the size of the pension scheme is too small to make a final salary scheme viable. Many employers are uneasy at the open-ended commitment implied by a final salary scheme, as this type of scheme is obliged to pay a pension at a known rate until the member's death, regardless of the state of the fund

---

Example

You are retiring at your normal pension age, and earn £30,000 a year. You have been a member of the pension scheme for 25 years, and the scheme's rules say that pension entitlement builds up on a 1/60 basis. After 25 years, the maximum pension allowed to you by the Inland Revenue is 25/60 of your final salary of £30,000; this would be a pension of £12,500 per year.

Your scheme's administrators have calculated that your pension fund will provide a pension of £10,000 a year. This is within the permitted limits. If the pension was greater than the limits, steps would have to be taken to reduce the pension, or if that was not possible, a refund would be paid to you, minus tax.

---

designed to pay for that pension. With a money purchase scheme, the commitment is related only to the fund which has been built up on behalf of the member. Once that fund has been used to provide a pension, the company has no further liability.

The actual benefits of a money purchase scheme vary from scheme to scheme – as long as they fall within the limits specified by the Inland Revenue. If you are a member of this type of pension scheme, the same advice applies as for members of final salary schemes: obtain a copy of your pension scheme handbook and study it carefully. If there are aspects of the scheme you still do not understand after you have read the handbook, seek advice from your pension administrator or an independent financial adviser. Remember that you have the right to a free copy of the scheme handbook while you are considering whether or not to join the scheme. The pension that you will enjoy is defined by the size of the fund you have built up over the years from both your own and your employer's contributions.

The scheme is obliged to provide you with an annual statement which gives some idea of the benefits you can expect at retirement or at death if you die before retirement age. The statement will be based on approved guidelines. Remember that this is only a guide – it does not promise that you

An annuity is an insurance policy. In return for the capital of your pension fund, the insurance company promises to pay you an income for life. The annuity's interest rate and the capital used to buy the annuity govern the size of the pension paid to you. The interest rate is calculated according to your age, sex and state of health, and also according to the investment returns which the insurance company can expect to make from the capital you have paid them.

> **Example**
>
> As a man of 65, you have a pension fund of £100,000 available to buy your annuity. This is after you have taken the lump sum allowed to you. Purchasing an annuity at an interest rate of 4% would produce an income of £9,631 a year for life. If the interest rate was higher, say 6%, then the annuity would pay you £11,109 a year for life.
>
> If you were a man of 60 with the same fund of £100,000, then the income at the two interest rates above would be £8,273 and £9,748: this is because actuarial calculations assume that you will live longer, taking the income from the annuity. For a man of 70, the income is more favourable at these interest rates – £11,501 and £12,990.
>
> Women are expected to live longer than men, and so the returns for them from annuities are lower. Again, based on the figures above, a woman of 65 would receive an income of only £8,061 at 4% interest, and £9,497 at 6%.
>
> **(Figures based on PA(90) actuarial tables.)**

will receive the pension described when you retire. This is because your fund will be used at retirement to buy an annuity, and the annuity provides your pension.

The annuities bought with the proceeds of a pension fund are called 'scheme' or 'compulsory' annuities, because you are obliged to buy the annuity with your pension fund. There are also annuities that are called 'purchased life annuities' (see Chapter 16).

If you take the option of a lump sum, then the annuity will be bought with the reduced fund available after the lump sum has been taken away.

Benefits

TAX-FREE LUMP SUM

If the fund is too small to produce a viable pension once the lump sum has been taken, or if taking a lump sum from a contracted-out scheme would leave a pension smaller than the SERPS-equivalent portion (see Chapter 4), then the lump sum may not be allowed, or the maximum size may be reduced.

The maximum lump sum is subject to the same rule as for final salary schemes; it cannot be more than 1·5 times the final salary earned. The methods of calculating final salary are the same: bonuses, overtime, commission and benefits such as company cars can be included, and the calculation can be made in one of two ways specified by the Inland

Revenue (see Chapter 5).

The rules relating to pensions you can provide for your dependants are the same for money purchase schemes as they are for final salary schemes:

○ A spouse or adult dependant can be paid a pension of up to two-thirds of the maximum pension which the member could have taken.

○ Other dependants can be paid pensions as long as the total pension paid does not exceed the maximum pension allowed to the member, and as long as no one dependant receives more than two-thirds of the total pension payable.

With a money purchase scheme, the survivor pension is arranged through buying a suitable annuity; this reduces the amount of pension paid to the member, as it would under a final salary scheme. The problem with money purchase schemes is usually that there is too little money available for survivor pensions to be generous.

Early retirement

VOLUNTARY EARLY RETIREMENT

If your company scheme is willing to allow you to retire early, you can do so from the age of 50. The calculations of the benefit you can receive are fairly simple, since the funds you have built up to the date of your early retirement are used to buy an annuity exactly as would have happened if you retired at the normal age.

However, you are limited by the Inland Revenue rules – if your scheme builds up entitlement at 1/60 for each year, and you have worked 20 years, then your maximum pension will be 20/60 of final salary. The pension you receive is based on the size of the available fund and your age. The main problem is that a younger person will have a smaller pension fund, and will be expected to live off the annuity longer than a person retiring at an older age. The rate offered by the annuity will therefore be lower, producing a much smaller annual income.

If your employer is unwilling to allow

> If you are likely to find yourself forced to take early retirement through ill health, it's very important to discuss the matter fully with your company's pension scheme administrator before you make a final decision.
> You could, perhaps, also talk to an independent financial adviser in order to get a second opinion.

you to take early retirement at the age that you would prefer, you can start a personal pension scheme and transfer your assets to it from your company scheme. This would allow you to specify your own retirement age in the personal pension. Usually, the transfer from a money purchase scheme to a personal pension will be straightforward, though you should still be aware that you may lose out financially in the transfer.

EARLY RETIREMENT THROUGH ILLNESS

If you are forced to retire early because of illness, then your position may be very poor, since your pension will again be based on the much smaller fund that you have been able to accumulate prior to your retirement. If your life expectancy is very short, then you may be able to buy an annuity from a firm specialising in this area – this is often referred to as 'impaired lives' – which will pay a much more favourable income because you are not expected to live very long. The Inland Revenue maximum pension allowed would be based on your entitlement if you had reached normal retirement age.

In cases where you retire early because of ill health, your company scheme may make discretionary payments, or cover may be available under the company's group permanent health insurance scheme.

Investment

MONEY PURCHASE SCHEMES

These are invested in the same sorts of ways as the assets of final salary schemes. The main difference between the two types of scheme is that in a money purchase scheme the assets are much more clearly earmarked for the individual member, and the investment approach is more tailored to the member's age and needs.

Investments for younger scheme members may be in equities, where a higher gain is likely, at the expense of greater risk of short-term losses. For older members, who are on the verge of retirement and who therefore cannot risk a short-term loss, the investments will more likely be switched into investments such as gilts, which produce less exciting investment gains but are much more secure.

Often the individual member will be able to involve himself or herself in the investment decisions, taking a role in managing his or her future pension. Or the process can be entirely handled by the scheme's administrators, if you prefer.

Example

If you were a healthy man retiring at 55, under current interest rates, you could assume that each £9 of your accumulated pension fund will buy £1 of pension a year.

At 65, the current rates would mean spending £7.40 of your pension fund to buy £1 of pension a year. This is because a man of 55 can expect on average to live another 22 years, and the annuity will have to keep paying a pension for the whole of that time. Current life expectancy for a man of 65 is 14 years – a much shorter time over which an income has to be paid.

If a man retires at 55 with a pension fund of £60,000, then the pension could be expected to be:

£60,000/£9 = £6,667 each year.

A man retiring at 65 with an identical pension fund could expect the following pension:

£60,000/£7.40 = £8,108 each year.

The other important difference to consider is that if you retire early you have less time to build up a pension fund. In this example, our man of 55 could build up a much higher fund if he waited until 65 to retire. If the contributions to his pension fund – from him and his employer – equal £2,000 a year, and if his fund grows at a rate of 8% a year (investment gains and interest), at 65 he could have a fund of approximately £160,000 to buy his annuity.

Using the same calculation as above, this would give him a pension of:

£160,000/£7.40 = £21,622 each year.

This example simplifies the calculation – it does not take into account inflation, or the likely increases in pension contributions from both employer and employee – but it does show the impact of early retirement on this kind of pension scheme.

Other types of money purchase scheme

TARGETED MONEY PURCHASE SCHEMES

These schemes behave in a way similar to a final salary employers pension scheme. A targeted money purchase scheme specifies the pension which the member can enjoy at normal retirement in terms of a percentage of final salary for each year of membership of the scheme – for example 1/60 for each year of service.

Contributions to the scheme will be regularly reviewed by an actuary so that the fund being accumulated is on target to provide the proposed level of pension.

If the fund is not sufficient to provide the targeted pension at your retirement, then additional funds will be provided in order to reach that target. These will come either from an unallocated part of the overall pension fund, or from special additional contributions from the employer.

There is one very important thing to be aware of in relation to this type of scheme. In a targeted money purchase scheme, the employer has made no promise that the proposed pension will be paid, so if circumstances change, the employer can avoid paying for those additional benefits; for example, this may happen if the company is struggling to stay in business.

In most normal circumstances, of course, an employer that has elected to set up a targeted money purchase scheme will not depart from that practice; as mentioned above, the employer is only likely to do so in cases of extreme difficulty. And even if it does, the basic benefits of the scheme will not be affected, and these will be equal to those under any normal money purchase scheme.

Where a targeted money purchase scheme stays on target, the advantage is that you can plan much more effectively for the future, since you know the likely pension at retirement. There will be less impact on the pension from the annuity rates prevailing at retirement date because if these are poor, the employer will provide sufficient funds to make up the difference.

INSURED MONEY PURCHASE SCHEMES

These are schemes where the investments are restricted to insurance policies. These policies provide the necessary cover, and build up an investment fund to pay for the individual's annuity purchase. They have a special temporary facility allowed to them by the Inland Revenue, whereby the member can delay buying an annuity, and take income from the pension fund instead. This would allow buying the annuity to be delayed at times when interest rates were low. The government intends to introduce this feature to all money purchase schemes in due course. Personal pensions already have this option (see Chapter 10 for more details, and a flowchart which illustrates the pros and cons).

Caution should be taken if you are considering delaying buying an annuity:

○ Taking income from the fund will deplete it. You could find that it is too small to buy a worthwhile annuity in the future.

○ Interest rates are not guaranteed to rise again when you want them to – they could even be lower in the future when you need to buy your annuity.

When you buy an annuity, you can't get the money back – and your family cannot inherit the fund when you die. If you've put off buying the annuity, the money remaining in the pension fund can be passed on to your heirs.

Pension deferral is a relatively new concept, so you need to talk through all the pros and cons with an independent financial adviser before making any decision.

Action plan

○ Check your scheme handbook for its exact definition of final salary.

○ What is the difference between this and the Inland Revenue maximum?

○ Does your scheme exclude bonuses or other benefits?

○ Does it make a deduction for the basic state pension?

○ If so, you have room to consider topping up your pension – see Chapter 14.

○ What is your scheme's retirement date?

○ Is that the date that you would like to retire?

○ Does your scheme allow early retirement, and, if so, on what terms?

○ If they are not favourable, you should look again at ways of topping up your pension (see Chapter 14) or make other savings for retirement (see Chapter 15).

○ Early retirement benefits can be unfavourable in a money purchase scheme – so think hard about ways of boosting your pension.

8 More employers pension schemes

Most pension scheme members in company schemes are members either of final salary schemes or money purchase schemes. There are a number of other types of employers pension schemes.

The uses of other types of employers pension schemes are normally quite specialised:

○ Certain types of schemes are designed for small companies.
○ Others are for company directors or senior members of staff.
○ Others are designed as means of providing pension cover beyond the maximum allowed under the Inland Revenue rules for exempt approved employers pension schemes.

GROUP PERSONAL PENSIONS

Where an employer is too small to consider setting up an occupational scheme, it may decide instead to consider a group personal pension. This looks in practice like a normal money purchase occupational scheme, but in reality it is a series of individual personal pension plans, one for each employee.

The employer usually collects the employee contribution in the normal way – via deductions from the payroll. The employer then adds any contributions it wishes to make, and forwards the whole amount to the firm providing the personal pension.

Whereas in a normal employers scheme, the scheme would decide on contracting out of SERPS, in a group personal pension scheme each individual has to decide. If an employee decides to contract out, the only difference is that the company will continue to deduct National Insurance contributions from salary at the contracted in rate: the rebate on National Insurance contributions will be paid by the DSS to the pension provider once a year.

The other big difference between an employers scheme and a group personal pension is that personal pensions have no limits imposed on the size of the pension which can be taken by the pension holder. Exempt approved employers schemes are limited to paying pensions of no more than two-thirds of final salary.

Personal pensions are not limited by the Inland Revenue; instead it limits the overall size of the contributions made to the pension plan, on an age-related scale. Employers pensions are not limited to an overall contribution level: the employee can contribute only 15% of salary, but the employer's contribution is not limited at all.

You should be aware that group personal pensions fall into a regulatory black hole. The personal pension provider is of course regulated, but there are no controls over an employer who operates a group personal pension on behalf of staff. There have been cases where unscrupulous employers have failed to pay over either the employees' contributions, their own, or both, to the pension provider. If you are in this type of scheme it is worth checking regularly with the provider that the contributions are being received.

For more details of how personal pensions work, and therefore of how a group personal pension would work, see Chapter 10.

Schemes for company directors and senior staff

Executive pension plans are money purchase schemes arranged with an insurance company; the contributions are used to buy insurance policies which fund the pension entitlements of the members.

They are designed to provide pension benefits for 'controlling directors' and other senior staff. Benefits accumulate for each individual in separate earmarked accounts within the main investment pool, rather in the way that benefits accumulate for individuals in normal money purchase schemes.

Independent financial adviser and *Moneywise* Ask the Professionals panellist Kean Seager says:

"The possibility of an employer making very substantial contributions makes these schemes very advantageous for senior staff. This is particularly true for people in their 40s or 50s who have made little or no pension provision in the past."

Controlling director

A controlling director is someone who was a director of a company in the ten years before retiring or leaving a company. This has to have been after 16 March 1987. He or she must have owned or controlled 20% or more of the company's ordinary share capital – this can have been by himself or herself alone, or in conjunction with associates. Associates in this instance include relatives, or trustees where the director (or a relative) has an interest in a trust.

Independent financial adviser and *Moneywise* Ask the Professionals panellist Kean Seager says:

"Small self-administered schemes have to be used wisely. The ability to self-invest in the company means that you can be hit with a 'double whammy' if the company fails. In those circumstances not only has your source of earnings gone west but your pension has suffered as well."

Most of the Inland Revenue restrictions on pension schemes also apply to executive pension plans. The maximum pension is two-thirds final remuneration, and survivor pensions can be paid subject to the same limits as normal occupational schemes.

The main difference in an executive pension plan is the level of funding which the employer puts into the scheme. It is usual for the employer to fund all of an executive pension plan. If you want to contribute, you're subject to the usual limit of 15% of salary. But the employer will contribute at a level far higher than it would for employees in its main money purchase scheme; in fact, unlike normal company schemes, the employer's contributions are limited by the Inland Revenue. The scale is age-related, and reaches 1,174.1% of annual remuneration for a married man aged 59 whose normal retirement age is 60!

SMALL SELF-ADMINISTERED SCHEMES (SSAS)

This is defined as being a scheme no larger than 12 members. Usually they will all be controlling directors, since there are considerable risks associated with the scheme. This is because a scheme like this is allowed a range of investment options which would be illegal for an ordinary employers scheme:

○ They can make loans from the pension fund for the purpose of the company's business.

○ They can invest in commercial property which can be used for the company's business.

○ The trustees can borrow money to buy an asset, such as commercial property, if the cost is more than the assets in the fund.

○ Schemes can invest in shares of unlisted companies, such as companies which do not have 'full' stockmarket listings and which therefore have not undertaken the rigorous process to achieve that listing.

There are stringent regulations which set limits on the above activities, and a list of activities which are specifically barred to a scheme of this nature.

The main attractions of a scheme of this type arise as a result of its ability to self-invest in the company which sets it up. This means it can benefit a small company and its directors, helping the business to grow in its expansionary phase.

Unapproved pension schemes

Although the name sounds a little alarming, unapproved pension schemes differ from approved pension schemes simply in that they do not enjoy any of the tax reliefs open to exempt approved pension schemes. The Inland Revenue uses the term 'top-up pension schemes' to refer to this type of scheme.

Unapproved or top-up pension schemes are designed to provide benefits for an employee who will already enjoy the maximum benefits allowed by the Inland Revenue under his or her main occupational scheme. They can only be used for employees – and not for the self-employed. The attraction of this type of scheme results from changes that have been brought about by the 1989 Finance Act:

○ The 1989 Finance Act introduced the concept of the earnings cap for post-89 members (see Chapter 5). High earners particularly suffer under the earnings cap, although given time almost all earners will be affected by it.
○ Prior to the 1989 Finance Act, members of an approved pension scheme could not enjoy its tax benefits if they were also members of an unapproved scheme. Since the 1989 Act this rule has not applied.

Employers can use unapproved pension schemes to boost the pension provision of employees who otherwise are on maximum Inland Revenue benefits.

The unapproved schemes do not enjoy the same tax concessions, but they can still be used to provide additional pensions on retirement. They are also occasionally used for employees who have completed the maximum qualifying service (usually 40 years) under the main company scheme. Rather than continuing to contribute to an approved scheme from which they can draw no additional benefits, they contribute instead into an unapproved scheme.

There are two main types of this scheme:

○ Unfunded unapproved retirement benefit schemes (UURBS): The benefits from the scheme are provided by the employer without a specific pension fund being set up. When a member retires, the employer then pays the pension on a 'pay-as-you-go' basis.

○ Funded unapproved retirement benefit schemes (FURBS): In this type of scheme the employer makes contributions to a specific pension fund, which is generally set up under a trust.

Because unapproved schemes do not enjoy the tax concessions that are allowed to approved schemes, there are tax liabilities relating to them:

○ The benefits from an UURBS are taxable only when the member or his survivors take them.

○ The contributions made by an employer to a FURBS are treated as a taxable benefit to you, the employee, and you pay income tax on them. On maturity, any lump sum will be tax free, but a pension will be treated as income, and taxed again!

Action plan

○ If you are in a small company which does not operate a pension scheme, ask the company if it will consider setting up a group personal pension and contributing to it. Failing that, ask if it will contribute to your own personal pension.

○ If you know that the earnings cap will affect you when you retire, or you know that you have no way of boosting your pension yourself, such as AVCs (see Chapter 14), ask your employer if it will contribute to an unapproved scheme on your behalf.

9 Moving jobs

If you move to a new employer, you need to review your pension arrangements. If you were a member of your old employer's scheme, you can leave the fund that has built up so far in that scheme – or you can take the money with you.

If you leave your current company scheme and not because you are retiring, then there are two options available to you:

○ You can leave the pension rights which you have accumulated in the company's pension scheme. This will be known as a 'preserved pension'. You can still join a new company's pension scheme, or start a personal pension, and this will not affect the preserved pension you have in your old scheme.

○ You can decide to have the pension rights which have accumulated under your old pension scheme moved to your new scheme if you join your new company's pension scheme, or take out a personal pension plan. This is known as a 'pension transfer'.

Independent financial adviser and *Moneywise* Ask the Professionals panellist Rebekah Kearey says:

"Your pension is automatically preserved until you decide whether to transfer it. There is no time limit for your decision and it is often better to wait a while before the best course of action can be ascertained. The decision is not final and can be reassessed every few years and especially in the five years before retirement."

Not so long ago, if you left your company scheme the options open to you were very poor. The pension which you left 'frozen' in your old employer's scheme was frozen in every sense of the word, losing its value in real terms year by year – the preserved pension was based on the salary you earned at the time you left. No allowance was made for the effects of inflation.

Even then, you might have been one of the lucky ones – some company schemes denied leavers any benefits from the employer's contributions. So the preserved pension was based only on the employee's own contributions, which would have been much smaller than those of the employer. If an employee took a refund on contributions instead, this might have represented a very poor return on the money he or she had paid into the scheme. The only protection was that a contracted-out pension scheme would have been required to make increases in the guaranteed minimum pension (GMP) – the SERPS equivalent. The situation today is very different.

LESS THAN TWO YEARS' MEMBERSHIP

If you leave your pension scheme before you have completed two years' membership, you are entitled to a refund of all the contributions you have paid into the scheme. Tax will be deducted from the refund by the Inland Revenue. This is because your pension contributions enjoyed tax relief when you made them – so the Inland Revenue claws back its 'cut' at this stage. If your scheme is contracted out of SERPS, an additional deduction will be made to reflect the reduced National Insurance contributions you paid while contracted out, and in order to 'buy' you back into SERPS.

TWO OR MORE YEARS' MEMBERSHIP

If you leave after two or more years of membership of your pension scheme, then the scheme must hold a preserved pension for you until your normal retirement age under the scheme rules. It will do this unless you choose to take a pension transfer to your next pension scheme. Your pension will be preserved at the point you had reached in your old company scheme.

Your preserved pension will then be increased each year to take account of the impact of inflation. Your old company scheme must increase the value of your preserved pension in line with the annual increases in retail price index – or 5% if that is lower.

At normal retirement age you will be allowed to take your pension under the same terms as if you had stayed in the company scheme until retirement. So if your scheme allowed a lump sum to be taken, you would be entitled to this, and also to the same level of survivor pensions as you would have had if you had stayed in the scheme. You will also be paid increases at exactly the same level as the scheme's other pensioners.

> **Example**
> If you had ten years of service, and your company scheme built pension benefits up at 1/60 for each year of service, your preserved pension will be 10/60 of final pensionable salary. In this case, final salary will be determined at the date you leave, based on one of the allowed methods of calculating the figure (see Chapter 5).

If your scheme is contracted out of SERPS, then the SERPS-related part of your pension must be treated according to special rules. With regard to pension rights built up before April 1997, employers can do one of the following:

○ Increase the GMP element of the pension in line with the published annual increases in national average earnings. These usually increase at a higher rate than the RPI.

○ Increase the GMP at a fixed rate, rather than following increases in national average earnings. This rate is set by the government, and is currently 7%. So if national average earnings increase faster than that rate, the employer saves; if they increase at less than that rate, the employee gets an additional benefit.

○ Limit their liability to an increase of 5%. The employer then pays a fee to the DSS, which in turn funds the balance of the increase over 5%. Obviously if earnings increase at less than 5%, the actual increase in earnings is used instead.

Pension rights built up after April 1997 are subject to different rules. The part of your final salary scheme pension which is treated as the SERPS equivalent is now called the Requisite Benefit. It must be revalued in line with RPI – not national average earnings – and there is a limit of 5% on this increase. So in fact the position for the SERPS-related part of your pension is worse after April 1997 than it was before.

The alternative course of action when you leave your existing company is to have the pension entitlement you have built up under your existing scheme transferred to a new scheme. This right has existed since January 1986. In theory, pension entitlements built up before January 1986 are not transferable, although most employers will include these rights when a pension transfer is made.

Pension transfers can be made into:

○ The new employer's scheme, if it will accept the transfer.

○ A personal pension, or a Section 32 'buy-out' policy. This can be done if the new pension scheme will not accept the transfer, or if the new employment is not pensionable. A Section 32 policy is an insurance policy designed only to hold the transfer value. It cannot receive other contributions. A personal pension on the other hand could receive a transfer, and also contributions from an individual who was not in pensionable employment.

Sadly, pension transfers are not straightforward, and even the best schemes can take a long time to carry out a transfer. They are complicated because of the differences which exist between different employers pension schemes, and often it will take a long time to establish a fair value for the transfer which is agreed by the two pension schemes involved.

Typically, when a pension transfer is requested, the pension scheme you are leaving will undertake the following calculation. As an underlying principle, the pension scheme is expected to make the calculation fairly, and will normally be expected to conform with guidelines laid down by the Institute of Actuaries:

○ The first step is to calculate the amount which the preserved pension would be worth at normal retirement age; this will include revaluations for future inflation. The scheme should use reasonable assumptions for these revaluations.

○ Next, the scheme calculates how much it would cost to buy an annuity which would pay the pension calculated in the first step. Again, the scheme has to use reasonable assumptions about the interest rates which might apply at that future date, since it is the annuity's interest rate which determines the pension paid for by that annuity.

○ Finally, the scheme has to work backwards to establish the amount of money required in today's terms to fund the purchase of that annuity in the future. The scheme has to make an assumption about the way in which the sum of money specified will grow through investment over the intervening years.

As you can see, the calculation is not straightforward, and there are a number of assumptions which the actuary making the calculation has to use; he or she has to decide on future increases in national earnings, inflation and interest rates, over a length of time which could easily be upwards of 30 years.

One of the most contentious aspects of the calculation made when deciding on the value of a pension transfer is the last part – how the actuary decides on the sum of money which will be needed to buy you that annuity in the future. If the actuary assumes that the money will be invested in line with yields in long-term gilts, then the sum of money transferred between the schemes will be larger than if the scheme actuary assumes that the money will be invested in shares. This is because shares generally produce better investment returns over the longer term than gilts – the same sum of money invested in shares will probably be worth considerably more in 20 or 30 years than if it had been invested in gilts.

So looking at it the other way round, if you know that in 25 years time you need to have a sum of £75,000 to buy an annuity, you can invest less in shares in order to produce that sum. If the actuary assumes a share-based investment when making his or her calculation, your pension transfer will have a smaller value than if the actuary had made his calculations assuming a gilt-based investment.

The Institute of Actuaries considers that the most appropriate way to carry out the calculation is by using the gilts-related method. However, in recent years more schemes have carried out the calculation based on the share-related method.

Another issue which can cause problems when pension transfers are calculated is that of discretionary increases. In the past, pension schemes were not obliged to increase the pensions which were being paid to pensioners. Only the SERPS-related part had to be increased. However, in practice most schemes make discretionary increases to help pensions keep up with the cost of living.

If your scheme expects to make discretionary increases on a regular basis in the future, then there is an argument for saying that the pension transfer value should contain an allowance for these future increases. But in practice this is so complex that, often, pension schemes do not make any allowances for future discretionary allowances.

The first thing to be aware of is that there is always some loss of pension entitlement when you transfer pension rights within the private sector. The new scheme may not match the benefits of the old scheme exactly, and the calculations used in valuing the transfer sum may also reduce it in comparison to what you would have enjoyed if the pension had remained preserved in the original pension scheme.

The only transfer between pension schemes which can be guaranteed to take place without any loss of benefit is between schemes which belong to the system known as the Public Sector Transfer Club. Schemes which used to be public sector, such as those in some of the privatised industries, can still take part in this system. The Public Sector Transfer Club system ensures that a pension transfer between club members provides a full credit from the old scheme to the new.

On the other hand, transferring your pension to a new scheme will allow you to receive all your pension from one source. You will have one retirement date, and one set of terms and conditions – perhaps an earlier retirement age than your old scheme. Your new pension scheme may improve its benefits, and may well include the transferred portion of your pension in that improvement. A preserved pension in your old pension scheme might not enjoy such favours.

Transferring from a final salary scheme to a personal pension or a money purchase scheme could produce better results in the long term, if the new scheme has an investment policy which produces better returns on your money. Of course, you should also be aware that there is more risk in such schemes – your return depends on the success of the investment, rather than a guaranteed return based on your final salary, so it is also possible that you could be worse off.

Many schemes – often the smaller ones – will offer you a fixed pension in return for the transfer value. This will be separate from the pension entitlement you will build up as a member of your new scheme.

Because of differences in scheme benefits, and also because the new scheme's actuary will have a policy for calculating the transfer value, the amount offered in a new scheme will never be precisely the same entitlement you would have had under the old scheme. Alternatively, your new scheme may allocate your pension transfer in the form of added years. Again there will probably be a disparity, and in this case it may be very obvious to you. You could find that in your old scheme you had ten years' pensionable service, which may be worth only seven or eight years in your new scheme.

If the new scheme is a money purchase scheme, the transfer sum will be added to the investment made by the new scheme on your behalf. The size of the final pension depends on the success of the new scheme's investment policy, and the interest rates which apply to annuities when the pension matures.

Action plan

○ Find out the forecast value of your preserved pension from your old scheme. Find out whether it would be included in future improvements to the scheme.

○ Find out from your old scheme the basis on which they will make the calculation of the transfer value and obtain a transfer value from them.

○ Find out how your new scheme will treat your pension transfer (see below). Find out also if a transfer will be included in any future improvements to the scheme (and find out at the same time if any improvements are planned or are in the pipeline).

○ If you are transferring between final salary schemes, you now have the information to decide on your course of action. You will be able to compare directly the projected value of your preserved pension against the value of the transfer you could make to the new scheme. If the preserved pension offers much better benefits, then you should take that option, unless you have good reasons for wanting to quit your old scheme altogether.

○ If you are transferring to a personal pension or money purchase scheme, you will need to assess the investment strategy of the new scheme. Is it likely to yield high investment gains, and consequently take the risks of short-term losses which will be inherent in that strategy? If so, then you need to consider what your own attitude to risk is. Would you be happy with that sort of approach?

If you have any doubt, or feel that you really do not understand all of the issues and risks involved, then discuss the matter with a qualified independent financial adviser.

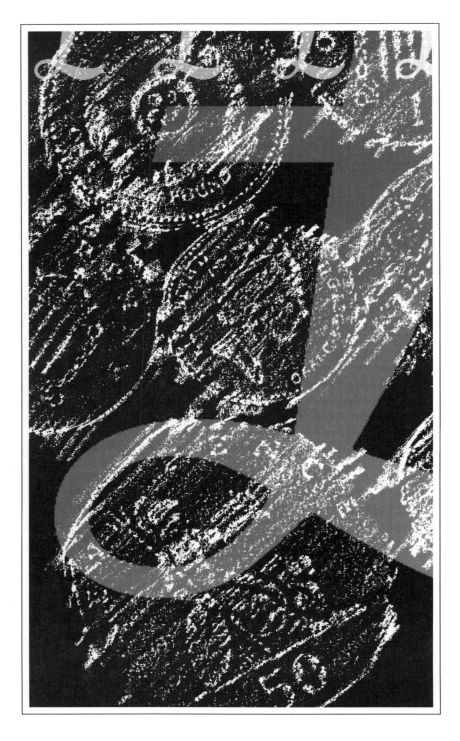

10 Personal pensions

Personal pensions are available for those people who cannot be members of company schemes – the self-employed and employees in companies which do not operate pension schemes.

You can also have a personal pension even if your company runs a pension scheme. Since 1988 employees have had the right not to join their employer's scheme, though you should consider the options very carefully before deciding not to join your company scheme (see Chapter 5).

Personal pensions work in the same way as money purchase employers pension schemes. Your contributions go into a fund which is invested on your behalf. At the retirement date specified when you set up the personal pension, the proceeds of the investment fund are used to buy an annuity.

The size of your final pension depends on:

○ The amount you contribute to the pension plan.
○ How successful the pension provider is at managing the investment on your behalf over the years.
○ Your age at the chosen retirement date, and your sex, since your life expectancy at retirement has a significant impact on the annuity rate you will be offered – and this in turn affects the size of your pension.
○ Investment conditions prevailing when you buy the annuity. If these are poor – during a recession, for example – the prevailing annuity rates will also be poor. Fortunately, there are concessions available to personal pensions which will allow you to try and minimise this last problem (see page 128).

Personal pensions were introduced in the Finance Act 1987 and came into being on 1 July 1988. Prior to that date, schemes known as 'retirement annuity contracts' existed. Retirement annuity contracts were similar to personal pensions, but were more restricted in their use. No new retirement annuity contracts were issued after 1 July 1988. If you have a retirement annuity contract from before that date, it can remain in force and you can still contribute to it (see page 129).

The main features of personal pensions are:

○ You can take a pension at any age between 50 and 75; you choose the retirement age when you set up the personal pension.

○ You can have more than one personal pension. It is common to have a series of personal pensions maturing at different ages, so that you can have a phased retirement – this is called segmentation.

○ You cannot pay into a personal pension, and also pay into an occupational pension scheme at the same time for the same employment. The exception is where you have a personal pension in order to contract out of SERPS, while being a member of an employers scheme contracted into SERPS. If you have income from two different employments, you can have a company scheme for one, and a personal pension for the other – see 'Income from more than one job' on page 119.

○ There is no limit to the size of the pension you can take from a personal pension. You can also take a tax-free lump sum of up to 25% of the fund built up in your pension plan.

○ You can contribute to a personal pension only if you have suitable earnings for the tax year in question.

○ Contributions to a personal pension are limited – as a proportion of the relevant earnings – according to your age.

○ Your employer can contribute towards a personal pension; this was not allowed under the terms relating to retirement annuity contracts.

○ Personal pensions can be used to contract out of SERPS; this was also not allowed under the terms relating to retirement annuity contracts.

You might be concerned about being able to afford regular contributions to a pension plan, particularly if you are self-employed and your pattern of income is irregular. You might not have the disposable income or the security to be able to commit to a regular monthly contribution to a pension plan. Most pension schemes therefore allow payments to be made in a variety of ways. You can make regular monthly contributions, or annual lump sums. You can vary the amount of a monthly contribution as necessary, paying more when you can afford it. You do not have to make any contributions whatsoever in a given year if you do not have the money to spare for your personal pension. The Inland Revenue allows personal pension holders the opportunity to catch up on missed contributions in later years through a system known as 'carry forward and carry back' (see later in this chapter, and Chapter 14).

Inland Revenue rules

To be able to contribute to a personal pension, you have to satisfy two conditions:

Independent financial adviser and *Moneywise* Ask the Professionals panellist Keith Sanham says:

"Look at the numbers: 8 contributions payable from the age of 19 to 26 produce a fund that is greater than deferring starting the pension to the age of 27 and paying every year to the age of 65; an outlay of £16,000 compared to an outlay of £78,000 and assuming a steady growth rate of 10% after charges. Start early!"

○ You have to be aged under 75 when you make the contribution payment.
○ You have to have 'net relevant earnings' (see page 118).

In addition, a personal pension can be used to receive funds from another pension scheme, for example, a transfer out of your previous employers scheme, another personal pension or a retirement annuity contract. An appropriate personal pension can also be used to receive the rebates paid by the DSS if you contract out of SERPS (see 'What contracting out means for your personal pension' later in this chapter).

RETIREMENT AGE

You can take the pension from a personal pension plan at any time between the ages of 50 and 75. You specify the age when you set up the personal pension, and you do not need your employer's permission. Also, you do not have to retire in order to take your pension. You can start to draw your pension and keep on working at the same time. Some occupations can retire at earlier ages which have been agreed with the Inland Revenue: footballers and dancers, for example, can retire at 35, and cricketers and trapeze artists can retire at 40.

Taking your pension from a personal pension plan is very similar to taking a money purchase employers pension. The fund will be used to buy an annuity, and there is the option to take a lump sum which would be tax free. The annuity bought must be payable for life. It can be guaranteed for up to ten years, which means that if you die within the period of the guarantee, the remaining income from the guaranteed period will be paid to your estate. The annuity must pay income to you at least once a year, either in advance or in arrears. The annuity can be:

○ Level – there will be no increases to your pension while it is payable.
○ Increasing – it can increase each year in an attempt to make sure that your pension keeps up with inflation.

More information about buying annuities can be found in Chapter 16.

Early retirement
This is not possible with a personal pension scheme, except for occupations of the type discussed above where the Inland Revenue has agreed special conditions. Instead, when you start your personal pension, you should consider very carefully the age at which you want to retire. Remember that a personal pension can mature at age 50 or older, so your early retirement can be built into the plan from the start.

If you are unable to continue your normal occupation, or an occupation for which you trained, as a result of illness or incapacity, you may be able to retire earlier than 50. You will need to have suitable medical evidence of your incapacity. In such a circumstance your pension scheme may allow you to take your pension early. In these circumstances, the same process applies as would have done if you had retired at the normal age. Your pension fund will be used to buy an annuity, which will provide a pension income for you. However, the income you receive may be small, and certainly will be much poorer than the pension you might have expected at normal retirement:

○ There will have been less time to build up your pension fund through contributions and through the investment gain.
○ Your life expectancy may still be quite long, and therefore the annuity will pay a less favourable rate than you could have expected at a later age, because the annuity will have to pay an income to you for much longer.

MAXIMUM PENSION

The big difference between employers pensions and personal pensions is that there is no maximum limit to a personal pension. The pension you take from your personal pension plan depends entirely on the factors outlined above – how much you contribute, how successfully the fund is

Age on 6 April	Maximum percentage of net relevant earnings
35 or younger	17.5%
36 to 45	20%
46 to 50	25%
51 to 55	30%
56 to 60	35%
61 to 74	40%

managed, your gender and chosen retirement age, and the annuity rate you buy.

Sadly, of course, there is a catch. In the case of personal pensions, the Inland Revenue stipulates maximum contributions to your pension each year (see above), so a personal pension works in the opposite way to an employers pension scheme.

In an employers pension, you can contribute only 15% of your earnings in any one year, while there are no limits to the overall contribution that your employer can make to your pension. Your maximum pension from an employers scheme is limited to two-thirds final salary. A personal pension is limited by the size of the annual contributions, but not in the size of the final pension payable.

MAXIMUM CONTRIBUTIONS

The Inland Revenue has specified limits on the amount you can contribute to your personal pension in any tax year. These limits apply to your net relevant earnings, and if these earnings are higher than the 'earnings cap' for that year, the earnings cap figure applies; net relevant earnings of more than £87,600 cannot be taken into account when contributing to your personal pension for 1998/99 (see page 119). The limits on contributions are age-related, and increase as you get older (see table above). So if you start your pension late, you have more opportunity to boost your fund with large contributions in the years you have left before retirement. The limits relate to your age at the start of each tax year on 6 April. When you reach 75 you have to take your personal pension, so contributions stop at the age of 74.

If you are employed and your employer contributes to your personal pension, then your employer's contributions are added to your own contributions, in order to make sure that they do not exceed the permitted limits.

Net relevant earnings are earnings which are liable to tax in the UK, in the following categories:

○ Income – including bonuses and taxable benefits – which would be subject to UK tax under Schedule E. If you are an employee, then you are subject to Schedule E tax, which is normally paid through the PAYE system. Note that your net relevant earnings are your gross income through employment – the sum on which you pay tax.

○ Income from property which is related to your employment.

○ Income which can be taxed under Schedule D arising from a business or trade. You must deduct business expenses from this income, as well as any losses or capital allowances for which you are claiming. For a self-employed person, net relevant earnings are basically the profits on which you must pay tax.

○ Income from certain patent rights which are treated as earned income.

Net relevant earnings do not include pensions, state benefits or redundancy payments. There are also exclusions affecting company directors – so you are advised to consult a qualified financial adviser should you come into this category.

The concept of the earnings cap for all pension schemes was introduced by the government in th 1989/90 tax year. For employers schemes the earnings cap applies only to the category of scheme members known as post-89 members (see Chapter 5).

Unfortunately, the system for personal pensions works in a different way, and no one who has a personal pension can escape it. If you choose to make a payment to a personal pension for the current tax year, or for any earlier tax year in which you are entitled to make a payment (see 'Carry forward and carry back' later in this chapter and in Chapter 14), then the earnings cap will be applied to your net relevant earnings.

You cannot take earnings exceeding the earnings cap into account

Tax expert and *Moneywise* Ask the Professionals panellist Janet Adam says:

"Remember that you obtain tax relief on contributions to a personal pension scheme only if you have sufficient net relevant earnings in either that year or the previous tax year to use the relief available to you."

Example

You are a woman of 48 who works for a small business which does not run an employers pension scheme. Instead, your employer contributes to your personal pension. In the 1998/99 tax year which ended on 5 April 1999, you earned £24,000 from your employer, together with a bonus of £2,000. The bonus is taxable, so your net relevant earnings for the 1998/99 tax year are £26,000. This is well beneath the earnings cap of £87,600 for that year.

You are aged 48 now, and your birthday was on 20 May, so on 6 April 1998, at the start of the 1998/99 tax year, you were aged 47. At this age you can pay the equivalent of 25% of your net relevant earnings into your personal pension. So the total you are allowed to pay into your personal pension for 1998/99 is 25% of £26,000 – or £6,500.

Your employer has agreed to pay £2,000 into your pension for the year. That leaves a maximum contribution of £4,500 which you could pay into your pension yourself.

when calculating your maximum pension contribution. The table, below, shows the earnings caps which apply to each tax year since its introduction.

Income from more than one job
If you earn money from more than one source, this needs to be taken into account when calculating your pension contributions to a personal pension. You may work for an employer part-time, for example, and have a self-employed career at the same time:

The earnings cap	
1989/90	£60,000
1990/91	£64,800
1991/92	£71,400
1992/93	£75,000
1993/94	£75,000
1994/95	£76,800
1995/96	£78,600
1996/97	£82,200
1997/98	£84,000
1998/99	£87,600

❍ If you do not have an employers pension from any employment, then all of your earnings are aggregated to produce a total earnings figure. The earnings cap is applied to this figure, if necessary.

❍ If you are a member of a company pension scheme, and also have self-employed earnings, or earnings from an employer which is not associated with the first employer, then all of the earnings from your self-employment and/or the second employer can be used to contribute to a personal

Why should I worry about the earnings cap?

The earnings cap may seem very high to most people, but you should not disregard it completely:

○ Although the earnings cap is usually increased for each tax year, it does not have to be; it was not increased in the 1993/94 tax year. There is no guarantee that it will keep up with inflation.

○ Increases in the earnings cap are usually made in line with increases in the RPI. The RPI generally increases at a slower rate than national average earnings, so your earnings are increasing at a faster rate each year than the earnings cap which will be applied to them.

As a result of this, the earnings cap will probably affect most people in the course of time, unless the government makes changes to the way the cap applies.

pension. The earnings cap does not apply to the earnings from the pensionable employment (the employer whose pension scheme you belong to).

○ If you work for two employers that are associated in some way, then the rules are different. Associated means that one employer controls the other, or they are both controlled by a third party. Both sets of earnings have to be taken into account. If you are not a member of the pension schemes of either company, then the process is the same as in the first point above. If you are a member of one of the pension schemes, but not the other, the earnings relating to the pensionable employment must be deducted from the earnings cap. This may limit the amount of earnings from the second employer, which you can take into account for your personal pension. This is different from the second point above, where the two employers are not associated.

Tax relief

In the same way as with all contributions to Inland Revenue approved pension schemes, contributions to personal pensions enjoy full relief from income tax. The fund invested on your behalf also grows partly free of tax.

These concessions from the Inland Revenue are extremely generous, and form part of the reason why the Inland Revenue puts a limit on the size of pensions which individuals can build up, either by limiting the pen-

Calculator

How much can you contribute to your personal pension scheme?
Use this calculator to work out the maximum contributions you are allowed to make to your pension.

Employees   £

Annual salary (gross basic from payslip), plus

    Annual bonuses, overtime

    Profit related pay (gross)

Taxable value (from your P11D) of:

    Company car

    Private health cover

    Mobile phone

    Other benefits

Taxable earnings

Self-employed

Gross income

    Minus expenses

    Minus capital allowances

    Minus loss relief

Taxable earnings

Employees and Self-employed

If your taxable earnings are more than £87,600, write £87,600 in Revised Total Earnings below

If not, write your taxable earnings in Revised Total Earnings below

REVISED TOTAL EARNINGS

What was your age at the start of the current tax year?

What % of net relevant earnings can you contribute at your age?

sion itself in the case of occupational schemes, or by limiting the contributions which can be made in the case of personal pensions.

Individual contributions
Your contributions towards your personal pension enjoy tax relief at your top rate.

How the tax relief is given depends on whether you are an employee or whether you are self-employed. If you are an employee, then tax relief at the basic rate is claimed back by the pension provider on your behalf and credited to your pension plan; effectively, you make the contribution net of tax at the basic rate. If you pay tax at the higher rate, the tax relief must be claimed by notifying your tax office either by letter, or through your tax return; your tax code will then be adjusted to increase your tax-free income by the necessary amount.

If you are self-employed, you have to make your pension contributions gross; you cannot deduct tax relief at source. You then notify the Inland Revenue by means of your tax return, and are given relief through your tax assessment.

Employer contributions
If your employer contributes to your personal pension, these contributions combined with your own cannot exceed the allowed percentage of net relevant earnings for your age. The employer will receive full tax relief on the contributions which, like other business expenses, count as a deduction against company profits.

You are not liable for tax on the employer's contributions. In the same manner as employer contributions to a company scheme, they do not count as taxable benefits to the employee. Employer contributions cannot be made using either carry forward or carry back (see below).

Carry forward and carry back
If you are contributing to a personal pension scheme, it is possible that in certain years you won't contribute as much as you would like to, or as much as you are allowed. This is most likely to apply to the self-employed, whose earnings pattern is often irregular and uneven – in many years you will simply not have the disposable income to afford to

Tip
If you are a non-taxpayer, or pay tax only at the lower 20% rate, your pension contributions are still entitled to tax relief at the basic rate of 23%. The Inland Revenue will not attempt to claw back the difference.

Example

You earn £32,000 in the 1998/99 tax year. You are single and you were aged 37 at the start of the tax year. You have no taxable benefits and are entitled to the full personal allowance of £4,195 for 1998/99. If you pay nothing into your personal pension, your tax liability for 1998/99 is as follows:

Income	£32,000
Personal allowance	£4,195
Taxable income	£27,805
Tax at 20% (on the first £4,300 of taxable income	£860
Tax at 23% (on the next £22,800 of taxable income)	£5,244
Tax at 40% (on £705, the balance of your taxable income)	£282
Total tax	£6,386

If, however, you make a contribution to your personal pension of £4,500 for 1998/99, it will affect your tax liability as follows:

Income	£32,000
Personal allowance	£4,195
Pension contribution	£4,500
Taxable income	£23,305
Tax at 20% (on the first £4,300 of taxable income)	£860
Tax at 23% (on the balance of £19,005 of your taxable income)	£4,371.15
Tax at 40%	£0
Total tax	£5,231.15

Your tax bill will be £1,154.85 lower due to your pension contribution. In the first example, £705 of your income was liable to tax at 40%. In the second, this 40% liability has disappeared, so you have received tax relief at 40% on £705 of your pension contribution. The balance of the contribution received tax relief at the standard rate of 23%.

123

make a pension contribution.

To help holders of personal pensions make the maximum contributions to their pension plans, the Inland Revenue allows you to take advantage of contribution allowances which have not been fully used in previous years. There are two methods of doing this, and they can be used either separately or in combination:

○ Carry forward means that if you did not make the full contribution which the Inland Revenue allowed in one or more of the six tax years prior to the current one, you can make a pension contribution in the current year in respect of those previous years' allowances. This allows a much bigger contribution to be made to your pension in a year when you have surplus cash, and can make up for any previous years when you could not afford to pay into your pension.

○ Carry back means that you can make a payment to your pension in this tax year, and choose to have it treated by the Inland Revenue as if you had paid it in the previous year. This is useful if you were a higher rate taxpayer in the previous year, and only a basic rate taxpayer in this year. By using the carry back option, your contribution will benefit from tax relief at the higher rate.

This subject is covered in detail in Chapter 14.

Personal pension scheme benefits

Lump sums You will be allowed to take a lump sum of up to 25% of the value of the pension fund accumulated on your behalf.

If you are contracted out of SERPS, then that part of your pension fund which relates to your SERPS-equivalent pension must be excluded from the calculation (see 'Contracting out of SERPS' page 126). If your personal pension fund includes funds which were transferred from an employers pension scheme, those funds have to be excluded when calculating the lump sum.

For a small number of personal pensions, the rules work differently. If you took out your personal pension before 27 July 1989, consult your pension provider for details.

MAXIMUM SURVIVOR PENSIONS

Personal pensions can pay benefits to survivors from the proceeds of the accumulated pension fund in some circumstances. The process depends on whether a member dies before or after taking the retirement proceeds from the policy.

Death before 'retirement'

If you die before retirement and take the proceeds from your personal pension plan, then your survivors will usually be entitled to the value of the fund accumulated in your pension plan. This is usually paid as a lump sum to your survivors or to your estate. It can also be paid as a pension to the survivors.

The payment of a pension to a dependant must not exceed the pension which would have been payable to the member, had he or she taken retirement the day before death. In this case, the pension payable to the member is considered to be the pension payable if no tax-free cash had been taken – this produces a higher pension, as taking the lump sum reduces the size of the pension payable.

The dependant can take a lump sum only if the pension fund contains transfer payments which have come from an employers pension scheme or certain other schemes. In this case, the dependant can take a lump sum of up to 25% of that part of the fund, with the remainder being put towards buying an annuity.

> 'Retirement' in this context means that your personal pension has matured and that you have taken the proceeds as an annuity and/or lump sum. It is possible to have a matured pension plan – be 'retired' under this definition – and continue to work. It is also possible – under rules discussed in 'Deferring your annuity' later in this chapter – to postpone taking the annuity. The proceeds of the policy remain in the invested fund.

If the pension fund contains 'protected rights' – the part of the pension assumed to be equivalent to your pension if you had remained within SERPS – then that has special treatment. A spouse's pension must be paid from the protected rights, if the spouse is older than 45, or younger than 45 with dependent children.

Death after 'retirement'

Where the pension fund contains 'protected rights' arising from contracting out of SERPS, the protected rights portion must be used to fund a spouse's pension of 50% of the pension which the protected rights would pay to the member. The remainder of the personal pension fund can provide a pension for the survivors if this option is chosen at 'retirement', as part of the annuity purchase. The pension paid to the spouse must not be greater than the pension which was paid to the member.

DEATH IN SERVICE BENEFITS

Members of employers pension schemes can be paid a death in service benefit by their employers, under Inland Revenue rules. This includes life insurance of up to four times annual salary.

For workers with personal pensions, the Inland Revenue will allow a proportion of the contributions to be used instead to buy a life insurance policy. This policy will pay out if you die before your pension policy matures. The maximum age to which you can write the life insurance policy is 75.

The Inland Revenue will allow you to contribute up to 5% of your net relevant earnings to this type of life insurance policy. This 5% reduces the age-related maximum contribution to your personal pension.

> **Example**
> A man aged 39 with net relevant earnings of £27,000 can contribute a maximum of 20% of these earnings to his personal pension, but he also wishes to contribute to a life insurance policy, to protect his wife and children in case he dies before 'retirement'. He can pay 5% of his net relevant earnings into his life insurance policy, but this comes out of his 20% allowance, and means that he will not be able to pay more than 15% of his earnings into his personal pension plan.

Contracting out of SERPS

A specific type of personal pension, known as an appropriate personal pension, can be used in order to contract out of SERPS (see Chapter 4, page 51).

You cannot do this if you are a member of an employers pension scheme which is already contracted out of SERPS. Remember that SERPS applies to employees only – if you are self-employed, SERPS does not affect you.

If you decide to do this, you and your pension provider jointly complete a form APP1. This is then sent to the DSS: if the DSS receives the form within six weeks of the end of the tax year (by 17 May), the decision can take effect in that tax year. Otherwise it takes effect from the next tax year.

Your employer will continue to deduct National Insurance contributions from your salary in the usual way. The DSS pays a rebate of National Insurance contributions for both your contributions and your employer's directly to your personal pension. This is usually about six months after the end of the tax year to which the rebate applies.

Until the end of the 1996/97 tax year, the rebate was the same for all employees who used a personal pension scheme to contract out of SERPS, with the exception that employees older than 30 were allowed a small additional rebate. From the 1997/98 tax year, the rebate system for contracting out into a personal pension changed. The size of the rebate is now age-related, starting at 3·4% when you are aged 16, rising to 9% at age 46 and above. From April 1999, the rebates are being increased slightly to compensate for the effect of the pension fund no longer being able to claim tax credits on share dividends – see page 33.

WHAT CONTRACTING OUT MEANS FOR YOUR PERSONAL PENSION

As mentioned in earlier sections, the pension rights that relate to contracting out of SERPS are given special treatment and are known as protected rights. They must be kept in an appropriate personal pension, separate from the other pension funds accumulating in your name.

The main points about protected rights are:

○ The pension from them cannot be taken earlier than age 60, unlike your ordinary personal pension, which can be taken from age 50.

○ You cannot take a tax-free lump sum from the protected rights pension fund.

○ The pension must provide for a spouse's pension of 50% of the member's pension.

○ The pension must increase at either RPI or 3% – whichever is lower – for pension entitlements accumulated up to the 1996/97 tax year. Entitlements accumulated from the 1997/98 tax year must increase at RPI or 5%, whichever is lower. This is done by buying an annuity meeting those requirements.

Survivor pensions must be paid according to the rules of SERPS (see Chapter 4).

SHOULD YOU CONTRACT OUT OF SERPS?

This is a complex decision, and one which depends on your income, age and gender. The situation changed further as from the 1997/98 tax year, since the whole system of rebates has changed and the return on the pension fund was reduced due to the July 1997 Budget measures (see page 33).

From April 1999, the age-related rebates are being increased to compensate for the impact of the July 1997 Budget changes. But, for the 1998/99 tax year, the contracting-out decision varies according to the reponse of your chosen pension provider to the cut in investment return. Some providers have reduced their charges for 1998/99 in order to keep their plans competitive until the higher rebates kick in from April 1999; some already have low charges and reckon contracting out remains worthwhile through their plans. Other providers are suggesting that contracting out with them is not worthwhile for anyone in 1998/99. Get advice from your provider or an independent financial adviser before taking any action.

> Independent financial adviser and *Moneywise* Ask the Professionals panellist Keith Sanham says:
>
> "People were advised to contract out of SERPS in government-promoted enthusiasm for personal pension planning. But it is not appropriate for everyone."

From 1999/2000, the position is 'back to normal'. In the main, if you are already contracted out of SERPS, it is probably best to stay contracted out until your retirement, assuming the original advice to you to contract out was sound.

If you are not contracted out, then you should consider contracting out if: you are a man aged under 55 or a woman aged under 45 and you are earning at least £11,000 a year (or £9,000 if you are paying voluntary National Insurance contributions). You should also plan to keep the personal pension in force for two to five years. Once you have contracted out, you should usually stay contracted out.

The decision is not entirely straightforward, however, and so if you're considering contracting out, don't make the decision by yourself – contact an independent financial adviser. If you are already contracted out and are worried about whether you've done the right thing, double-check with an adviser.

Special features

Using your pension to pay off the mortgage: You can use a personal pension in the same way as you can link an endowment policy to a mortgage. The tax-free lump sum from the pension will be used to pay off the mortgage at the end of its term.

> The only reason to contract out of SERPS is if the pension generated from the National Insurance contributions rebate is greater than the pension you would have been entitled to if you had stayed in SERPS.

With an endowment-linked mortgage, you take out an endowment policy, which is an investment-linked life insurance policy. This should build up capital during the term of the mortgage to pay off the loan. The life insurance cover will pay off the loan if you die before the end of the term.

With a pension-linked mortgage, you take out a personal pension, which is designed to mature at the time the loan needs to be repaid. The personal pension needs to grow sufficiently by the end of its term so that the lump sum can pay off the loan. You also have to take out separate life insurance, to pay off the loan if you die early; the personal pension will not have this protection.

There are a number of concerns with pension mortgages:

○ Personal pensions cannot be written to mature earlier than age 50, which could cause a problem for a younger borrower.
○ Only the tax-free lump sum can be used to pay off the mortgage. The maximum size of a tax-free sum is 25% of the pension fund accumulated. Using a pension to pay off a mortgage will therefore commit you to building up a pension far greater than you may require, and the costs in terms of pension contributions may be much higher than paying off a different kind of mortgage.
○ The tax-free lump sum is intended to be used to assist retirement, and committing it to paying off a mortgage may not be in your best interests.

The Inland Revenue has indicated that it is unhappy with the use of pensions to fund mortgages. The primary purpose of a pension is to provide a fund for an individual's retirement.

DEFERRING YOUR ANNUITY

You could take out a personal pension, or transfer into one, which allows you to defer buying an annuity to any time before you are 75. There are special rules which allow you to take an income from your pension but delay the commitment to an annuity. Once you buy an annuity you are generally stuck with the prevailing interest rates for life. By deferring the purchase you could wait until things improve (see Chapter 16).

The flowchart on page 130 shows what can happen if you buy an

Pension fund withdrawal *vs* buying an annuity

Source: Scottish Amicable

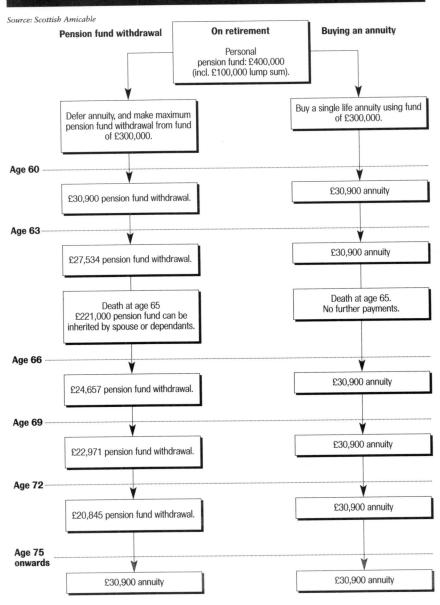

Pension fund withdrawal

On retirement

Buying an annuity

Personal pension fund: £400,000 (incl. £100,000 lump sum).

Defer annuity, and make maximum pension fund withdrawal from fund of £300,000.

Buy a single life annuity using fund of £300,000.

Age 60

£30,900 pension fund withdrawal.

£30,900 annuity

Age 63

£27,534 pension fund withdrawal.

£30,900 annuity

Death at age 65 £221,000 pension fund can be inherited by spouse or dependants.

Death at age 65. No further payments.

Age 66

£24,657 pension fund withdrawal.

£30,900 annuity

Age 69

£22,971 pension fund withdrawal.

£30,900 annuity

Age 72

£20,845 pension fund withdrawal.

£30,900 annuity

Age 75 onwards

£30,900 annuity

£30,900 annuity

annuity or opt for pension fund withdrawal. The better option will depend on several factors. The figures quoted assume annuity rates based on gilt yields of 8%, and investment growth of 9% after charges.

SEGMENTING YOUR PENSION

An option when setting up your personal pension is to set up the pension from the outset as a series of related pension plans; this is known as 'segmenting' the plan. Most providers allow this within the structure of an overall plan.

The main benefit of segmenting your pension is that the different segments can be written to mature at different ages. This can be designed to suit you and your retirement needs, providing, for example, a way of phasing in your retirement which allows you to take things easy in the last years of work.

The advantage of this approach is that the funds which mature later have longer to benefit from investment gains. On top of that, your age at the time you buy the annuity affects the interest rate paid: the older you are, the better it should be, because your life expectancy will be shorter. This approach can be very flexible, and each segment can of course be deferred when it matures, if annuity rates are poor when you wish to take the benefits from that segment of your pension plan.

What are the risks of segmenting your pension?

These are very similar to those discussed under the deferral option above:

○ The parts of your pension fund which are still invested could still suffer from a bad upset, if the investment returns worsen or share prices fall significantly.

○ There is no guarantee that annuity rates will continue at their same levels. Even where they are poor, it is possible that they could get worse.

On top of that, segmenting your pension plan into pensions which mature at different ages means that you cannot take a tax-free lump sum of the whole pension fund – you can only take a lump sum from the seg-ments which have matured. So if you know that you will have a need for the lump sum on retirement, this phased approach to your pension may not be suitable.

Again, there are advantages and disadvantages to this approach to your pension. You should consider all the factors very carefully, including the risks and your attitude to those risks, and if you are in any doubt, you should consult an independent financial adviser.

Other personal pensions

Self-invested personal pensions (SIPPs) These are personal pensions where you can manage your own investment strategy, or appoint a fund manager to carry out the strategy. Investments can be made in a wide range of securities.

You're not allowed to 'self-invest' or make loans to anyone connected with yourself. Self-investment would be using the pension funds to support your business. However, the pension fund can be invested in commercial property, which can be rented to your business. The rent, of course, accumulates in the pension fund tax free.

SIPPs are a specialised area, and if you are considering such a course of action, you should take independent financial advice.

RETIREMENT ANNUITY CONTRACTS

Although no new retirement annuity contracts can be taken out, holders of existing ones can continue to contribute to them. Retirement annuity contracts are similar to personal pensions; in each case the contributions are used to build up an investment fund which will be used to buy an annuity at retirement. The annuity will provide the pension income. A tax-free lump sum may be taken from the pension fund, leaving a smaller fund remaining with which the annuity can be bought. The contributions are fully entitled to tax relief, and the investment fund grows free from tax liability.

There is no earnings cap on retirement annuity contracts. Unlike the regime which applies to personal pensions, if you pay into a retirement annuity contract, you can take all of your income into account, and you do

Example
You can set up your pension plan in four segments to mature at 50, 55, 60 and 65. In this way your pension starts at age 50, and builds to its maximum over the next 15 years. In that time you can continue working, but can take things progressively more easily as your pension is supplementing your earnings.

Independent financial adviser and *Moneywise* Ask the Professionals panellist Kean Seager says:

"The wide investment powers of a SIPP and the ability for investors to manage their own investments can be real advantages. However, the investors must know what they are doing. Poor investment decisions can prove very costly to the fund."

LIMITS ON RETIREMENT ANNUITY CONTRACT CONTRIBUTIONS	
Age on 6 April	% of net relevant earnings
aged 50 or under	17·5%
51–55	20%
56–60	22·5%
61–74	25%

not have to disregard that part of your income which exceeds the earnings cap.

Retirement annuity contracts are subject to a different set of limits on the amount of net relevant earnings which can be taken into account. The scale is still age-related, but the percentages allowed are lower (see table above). It is possible to contribute to both a personal pension and also a retirement annuity contract in the same year, but if you do, the maximum contribution you make – across both plans – will be subject to the limits applying to personal pensions, including the earnings cap.

It is important, therefore, to be aware of the different rules relating to contributions, since at certain ages, and with certain levels of net relevant earnings, you may be better off putting all your contributions into a personal pension. At other ages and levels of earning, the opposite applies. If you are unsure what to do, consult your accountant or an independent financial adviser.

There are other important differences:

○ Tax relief on retirement annuity contracts is usually obtained through a tax assessment. So it can take longer to benefit from the tax relief. Employees can benefit from tax relief through PAYE.
○ Your employer cannot contribute towards a retirement annuity contract.
○ Retirement annuity contracts cannot be used to contract out of SERPS.
○ You cannot transfer the pension entitlements from occupational pensions, free standing AVCs or personal pensions into retirement annuity contracts; they can only receive transfers from retirement annuity contracts.
○ You can only take a pension from a retirement annuity contract from

133

Example

You are a woman aged 47 at the start of the 1998/99 tax year. You have net relevant earnings for the year of £110,000. You have a retirement annuity contract, and you also have a personal pension.

Under retirement annuity contract rules, a person aged 47 can contribute 20% of net relevant earnings into a retirement annuity contract. The earnings cap does not apply, so you can take all of your £110,000 net relevant earnings into account. The maximum contribution you can make to your retirement annuity contract is £22,000.

But if you want to contribute to your personal pension, the rules are very different. Although you can contribute a higher proportion of your net relevant earnings to your personal pension – 25% rather than the 20% allowed for a retirement annuity contract – the earnings cap of £87,600 means that you must ignore the final £22,400 of your net relevant earnings. The maximum you can therefore contribute to your personal pension is £21,900.

If you want to contribute to both your personal pension and your retirement annuity contract in the same tax year, then the personal pension limits apply to the combined contributions across both plans. You will be limited to a contribution of £21,900 – even if the bulk of that contribution goes into your retirement annuity contract.

the age of 60.

○ You cannot take income from your retirement annuity contract without buying an annuity. With a personal pension, new rules allow you to postpone buying an annuity and take income from the pension fund instead (see 'Deferring your annuity purchase' above).

If you have an existing retirement annuity contract, there are good reasons to continue to hold it and contribute to it, especially where you can contribute more to a retirement annuity contract than to a personal pension. If you are uncertain about the best course of action, consult an independent financial adviser.

Should you have a personal pension?

When a personal pension is right for you As discussed above, if you are a member of a company scheme, it is very unlikely that you will be better off taking out a personal pension.

> Once again, if you have any doubts about what to do, consult a qualified independent financial adviser. Getting it wrong can be very costly.

Even if your company scheme does not have the benefits which suit you, you should consider your position very carefully:

○ If you want to retire earlier than your company will allow, there may come a point when it benefits you more to leave the company scheme and start a personal pension written to the earlier retirement age. But it is also worth negotiating hard with your company scheme to get it to agree to your earlier retirement date.

○ Many company schemes will pay pensions only to your husband or wife; very few recognise unmarried partners, despite the fact that 'common law' partners have far more legal rights than they used to. And even fewer schemes recognise unmarried partners of the same sex as the member. But if your scheme will not pay out a survivor pension to your partner, that is not necessarily a reason to leave. By the time you retire, practice and legislation are likely to have gone a long way towards equalising the situation. Stay in your company scheme and lobby for changes to it – and only consider leaving the scheme and taking out a personal pension closer to retirement if you are certain that your scheme will not pay your partner a pension.

You should consider taking out a personal pension if:

○ You are self-employed.
○ Your company does not run a pension scheme.
○ Your company scheme is very poor; the benefits accrue at a very low rate, or your employer's contributions are low. Even then take advice before leaving your scheme.

If you are considering becoming self-employed in the future you should consider:

○ Staying in your company scheme until you actually start your self-employment.
○ Starting a personal pension when you leave a company to become self-employed; you can decide then whether to transfer the pension rights from your company scheme to your personal pension, or whether to leave them in the old scheme as a preserved pension.

MIS-SELLING OF PERSONAL PENSIONS

Between the introduction of personal pensions in 1988, and June 1994, a large number of people were advised to leave their employers pension schemes and transfer their pension entitlements to a personal pension instead. Others were advised not to join a company pension scheme, but to take out a personal pension. Eventually the financial services regulators became worried by the growth in this business, and were concerned that a considerable proportion of these people had been wrongly advised by advisers who had not taken the full facts into account.

The result of this is that the pensions industry is currently reviewing all pension opt-outs which took place between 29 April 1988 and 30 June 1994. Each case will be examined to see if the advice given at the time of the sale complied with the rules financial advisers were supposed to follow. An assessment will then be made to see whether the individual has suffered financial loss as a result of either leaving or not joining their company scheme. A loss will be considered to have occurred if the individual would have had a better pension as a member of the company scheme.

Among other things, the review will take into consideration:

○ Personal and survivor pension benefits.
○ Early retirement options.
○ Increases to pensions in payment.
○ Levels of contribution to the pension scheme, including employer contributions.

Given the view of the regulators, there is a strong possibility that in most cases opting out of the company pension will have produced a loss. The review will then decide whether or not the adviser's failure to comply with the rules was the cause of the loss.

If the review decides that the loss did result from the failure of an adviser to comply with the rules, the intention is to compensate the individual investor, either by reinstating them into their company scheme with the pension entitlements they would have otherwise enjoyed, or by topping up their personal pension to make good the

> **Be aware!**
> It is now the view of the regulators, led by the Financial Services Authority, that the decision to opt out of a company scheme, based on a full appraisal of the facts and suitable advice, is likely to be the exception rather than the rule.
>
> Opting out of an employers pension scheme is assumed by the regulators to be against the interests of the individual concerned, and the onus is on the financial adviser to demonstrate a convincing case of why a person should opt out.

Independent financial adviser and *Moneywise* Ask the Professionals panellist Rebekah Kearey says:

"Sadly many individuals were wrongly advised to transfer out of company pension schemes in the late 1980s. Nurses and teachers moved out in droves, most commonly because of an over-simplistic view of the forecasted benefits."

loss. The industry has been criticised for dragging its feet over the review process – and some pension providers are now using a short-cut system to work out whether someone is entitled to compensation. Several household name pension providers have missed the various deadlines for handling cases and subsequently were fined.

Action plan

○ If you do not have a pension, and cannot join an employers scheme, start a personal pension as soon as possible.

○ If you are able to join an employers scheme and have not done so, you should almost certainly join that scheme, rather than starting a personal pension.

○ If you are already in an employers plan, do not transfer out of that plan into a personal pension unless there are extremely good reasons for doing so.

○ Take care in deciding on the retirement age you want. Segment your plan if necessary in order to phase your retirement over a number of years.

○ Make sure that you take full advantage of the rules for carry forward and carry back. You will boost your pension and benefit from tax relief on the contributions.

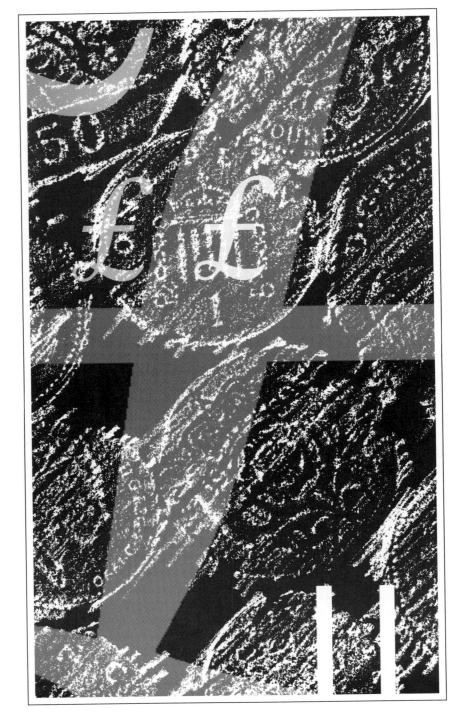

11 Choosing a personal pension

If you have come to the conclusion that the right course of action for you is to take out a personal pension, the next big decision is which personal pension to choose.

There are literally hundreds of pensions out there – how do you decide between them?

Your financial adviser will no doubt have clear ideas about which pension scheme you should buy, but how do you know the adviser is giving you the best advice? After all, he or she probably stands to make a considerable amount of commission as a result of your purchase. The next chapter deals with the process of choosing a financial adviser.

A pension is a long-term investment – you will probably be paying into it for 20 to 30 years. You need to be absolutely sure that your money is being used to its best advantage; poor investments, or high charges will eat into your returns. And when your returns dictate the amount of money you will have to live on in retirement, buying the wrong pension can prove to be a very costly mistake indeed.

When choosing a personal pension plan, you need to evaluate the following aspects:

○ Choosing a provider which offers the particular type of pension that suits all your requirements – in terms of when and how you retire, the type of pension you take (fixed or increasing, for example), and also what it provides for your dependants.
○ Choosing the investment mix which suits you.
○ Choosing a provider which can produce good investment returns for your money.
○ Choosing a provider with reasonable charges.
○ Choosing a provider which does not penalise you unduly for transferring your pension to another provider.

Which type of personal pension?

The first thing to do is to make certain that you know what you want to achieve:

❍ When do you want to retire?
❍ Do you want a pension which pays out all at once, or do you want to stagger your retirement, and therefore segment your personal pension plan when you buy it?
❍ Do you want a pension which stays level until you die, or one which will increase each year, in an attempt to protect you against the effects of inflation (an escalating annuity)?
❍ Do you want your pension to pay a pension to your spouse or partner when you die? Do you want to provide for pensions for dependent children?
❍ Do you want a guarantee that your pension will be paid for at least five or ten years, so that if you die before that time, your survivors will still benefit?

Be clear what you want, before you talk to a financial adviser or pension provider. Extra features cost money, which translates into a smaller pension when you retire. Do not be pressurised into paying for features you do not really want.

If you are unsure, or think your circumstances will change in future, buy a flexible product, which will allow you to add or take away features between now and the time when you take your personal pension. Two features you might want to consider are:

❍ *Waiver of premium:* This means your contributions will still be made if you are too ill to work.
❍ *Open market option:* All new personal pensions have this facility; it means you can opt to take your pension from a different provider when you get to retirement, see page 193.

The younger you are, the more you can afford to take a risk with your investments because you have a longer time to build your pension. Because of that, you can afford to risk short-term losses in your invest-

Personal pension checklist

I want to retire at age

I want to retire over a period, from age   to age

I want my pension to increase in order to keep up with inflation.   Yes/No

I am married/single/divorced/living with someone to whom I am not married.

When I die, I want my pension to pay a survivors pension to:

    ○ my spouse or partner

    ○ my children

I want to guarantee that my pension will be paid for:

    ○ five years

    ○ ten years

    ○ no guarantee

I want to pay a fixed amount each month into my pension.

I want the flexibility to pay monthly or annually, and to vary my contributions according to how much money I have. I want to be able to suspend payments altogether for a period if necessary.

I want to make sure contributions would still be paid if I were too ill to work.

My attitude to risk is:

Low risk
    I do not want an investment which could lose money.
    I will accept modest investment gains in return for peace of mind.

Medium risk
    I am prepared to risk some investment losses.
    I hope that I will enjoy better investment gains as a result.

High risk
    I am prepared to risk considerable investment losses.
    I hope that I will enjoy very high investment gains as a result.

ments, in return for a higher gain in the long term. Remember, you should only take a risk if you are comfortable with it. If not, invest in low-risk securities.

Which types of investment?

There is a wide range of personal pensions available, to meet the widely different needs of the public. The mix of investments in each is designed to produce a different rate of return. It is fair to say that the higher the rate of return, the greater the risk.

Personal pensions can be bought from insurance companies, banks and building societies, and from more specialised investment companies such as unit trust companies and investment trust companies. They are designed in one of two ways:

○ As 'with profits' insurance policies.
○ As unit-linked products, for example based on a unit-trust fund or similar.

'WITH PROFITS' INSURANCE POLICIES

Personal pensions based on this type of product work on a basis very similar to insurance company endowment policies. You have a guaranteed rate of return on the investment, usually modest at the outset.

The funds are placed cautiously, with a high proportion of interest-paying investments such as government stocks (gilts). At the end of each year, the pension is paid a bonus. The size of the bonus depends on the investment success of the fund, although the managers 'smooth' the bonus rate over good and bad investment years. In other words, the company keeps some money in reserve during good years to pay out in bonuses in years when investment performance is disappointing. Once you have been given a bonus, it cannot be taken away, and so it boosts the guaranteed amount you will receive at the pension's maturity.

There will usually also be a bonus paid at the end of the pension's life – a terminal bonus (also called a maturity, final or vesting bonus). This is not guaranteed, but can be a very significant proportion of your final fund.

'With profits' policies can be based on unit-linked funds. The principle of the investment is the same, although the charges may work differently

Unit trusts

With this type of investment, your contributions are used to buy 'units' in an investment fund. The contributions of all the other investors in the fund are treated in exactly the same way. The total fund can buy a wider range of investments than your individual contributions could, so the risk is spread more widely, and the potential for gain is increased. When you want to realise your investment, the fund manager buys back your units, and sells them to new investors. The value of the units when you buy and sell them reflects the performance of the whole fund.

Some unit trusts are converting to open-ended investment companies (OEICs). These are similar to unit trusts but have a simpler price and charging structure.

Investment trusts

These are similar to unit trusts, except that your contributions are used to buy 'shares' in the investment trust company. For the investor the mechanics are exactly the same as buying and selling units in a unit trust fund. The range of investment options open to an investment trust company is slightly wider than the range available to a unit trust. Very few personal pensions are offered via investment trust companies.

(see below), and the fund managers perform less 'smoothing' of the bonus rate; it will fluctuate more between good and bad years.

UNIT-LINKED POLICIES

These are based on unit trusts or investment trusts (see above). There is no guaranteed minimum, and no annual bonus. These policies therefore carry a higher risk than 'with profits' policies. The investment return at maturity depends on the sale price of your units – and this in turn depends on how well the fund is doing at that particular time. However, in return for that higher risk you have the potential of greater returns. Because there is no guaranteed return, the fund can choose from a wider range of investments, and can take advantage of markets which a with profits policy would avoid.

Different funds are set up to exploit different markets. Some specialise in very high-risk areas, such as the Far East, or the small companies sector. Others are more cautious, investing in European or North American shares. Others invest only in UK shares or fixed-interest investments. At the cautious end of the scale, investment returns will be similar to those of with profits policies.

Many pension providers have their own range of funds. Most companies allow one switch each year free of charge, with a small administrative charge for additional switches, so you can start off in a fund which has a higher-risk profile, and then switch your investment at a later stage to a more secure fund, to avoid losing money in the years when you are approaching retirement.

Which pension provider?

This is the trickiest part of all when you are choosing a personal pension. To get the best from your pension, you need to get the best returns on your investment, taking into account your attitude to risk.

The problem is that different companies can produce widely different rates of return from the same types of investment. It all depends on the quality of the fund managers – the best can identify opportunities which are missed by the poorer managers.

The problem is that the only thing to go on is the past performance of the pension providers. This gives an indication of how well their fund managers have performed in the past, but that is no guarantee that they will continue to perform equally well in the future. After all, fund managers who have been responsible for a company's past success may easily move to another company in the future, or retire.

However, while past performance is not a guarantee of what will happen in the future, a company which has shown good and consistent performance in the past is more likely to continue to have good and consistent performance in the future. A company which has had a few years of excellent performance, but which has otherwise had mediocre or poor performance, is more likely to be dependent on one or two 'star' fund managers, and hence it is more likely to suffer in the future if those star players leave.

There are a number of magazines such as *Money Management* and *Planned Savings* – designed for financial services professionals – which regularly publish performance tables of the different providers. These track pension providers over a long period of time. The problem is that they are difficult to follow if you do not work in this field. Choice of provider is a decision which often involves an independent financial adviser.

STOCKMARKET UPS AND DOWNS
The 'Stockmarket Ups and Downs' graph opposite shows how the share

144

STOCKMARKET UPS AND DOWNS
The Barclays Capital Indices

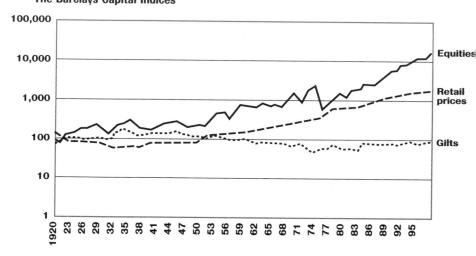

market – the risky end of the investment spectrum – has been performing since 1920. The ups and downs – some of them very dramatic – do not, however, mask an overall upward trend. The longer-term tendency for markets to beat inflation is also clear, though you can see that, during some shorter periods, inflation would have won the battle.

Charges

Whenever you buy an investment policy, you should be aware that not all of your money will go towards the investment itself. Part will go to cover the charges made by the provider for setting up and administering the pension plan.

Part of your contributions may also go to paying the person who sold you the policy. We will discuss how the salesperson is paid in Chapter 12.

In the past, the way charges were levied on investment products was the subject of much criticism because the charges were not clearly declared up front, and it was difficult if not impossible to work out what they were. Now the situation is different. Since 1995, financial services regulators have required that you are sent a 'Key Features' document (see page 146)

145

Key features document

This should be tailored to your individual requirements, although in some circumstances – the selling of investment policies by direct mail for example – the document can make reference to a 'typical' buyer of the policy or plan.

The Key Features document sets out:

○ What the product is, and what its purpose is.

○ The features of the product, such as bonuses and life insurance cover.

○ The risks associated with the policy.

○ What your commitment is.

○ The commission which will be paid to your financial adviser, if you have used one.

○ The charges made for setting up and administering the policy. This may be very clearly stated, or it may be in the form of a table showing the impact of charges over the life of your policy. It should also show you how much money you could lose if you surrender the policy early.

○ Projected investment returns according to specific percentage rates set out by the regulators; these are not necessarily the investment returns you can expect. Because these projections have to use standard rates of return they ignore the fact that one company may have a better record of fund management than another. Instead, they allow you to see clearly the effect of commission and charges made.

when you are in the process of buying an investment policy. This document must set out all the charges which the provider makes, enabling you to make a full comparison of the costs of different products.

The charges made cover the cost of setting up and administering the policy. Set-up charges cover both the company's internal administration costs, and also any costs associated with buying the initial investment. The charges may not appear high, but remember the length of time over which you are likely to hold your pension fund. If you are paying 1% to 2% of your pension fund in charges each year, then over 20 years those charges will eat up a considerable proportion of your total fund. So before you actually buy a pension plan it is important to shop around and compare charges.

If you take out a personal pension, and decide five or ten years later that you would have been better off with another provider, you may then discover that you cannot transfer your existing fund to a new provider without incurring penalties from your present provider. It is worth finding out from the outset what the penalties are likely to be. Hopefully, you will not have to take this course of action, but it is best to know what it will cost you in the future, if you decide that you have to transfer to a new provider.

Action plan

If you are considering starting a personal pension:

O Draw up a list – based on the checklist at the start of this chapter – outlining exactly what you want from your pension.

O Contact a range of pension providers directly to find out whether they match your criteria. Or consult your financial adviser to obtain the same information. Make sure the pensions have the flexibility to allow you to switch your investments to lower-risk funds as you approach retirement.

O The companies you contact should be firms with a good investment track history, and should be companies with whom you feel comfortable. Remember, you will be investing a considerable amount of money with them. Look out for surveys of past performance in newspapers or in magazines such as *Money Management* and *Planned Savings*. Consult a financial adviser if you do not feel entirely confident about doing this yourself.

O Make sure you understand the provider's charges and penalties.

As you can see, the process is not simple. Unless you are confident that you know what you are doing, you should consult a qualified independent financial advise ryou can trust. The wrong adviser can cost you dearly, and there is no guarantee that you would be able to get any recompense in the future for poor advice given today. The next chapter will help you choose the right financial adviser.

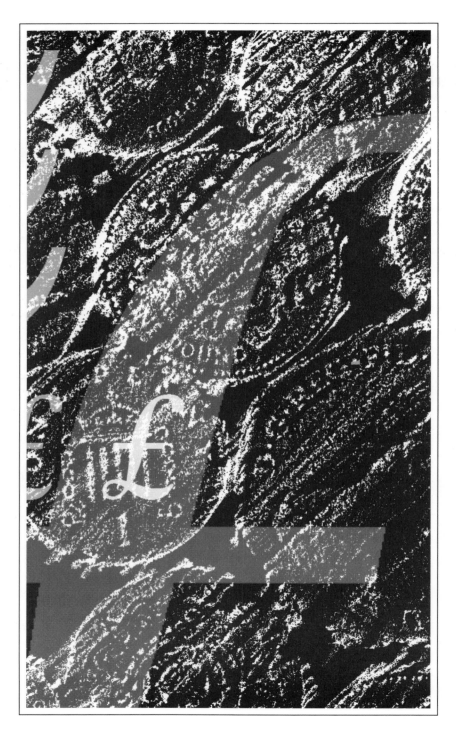

12 Getting advice

This book has repeatedly stressed that if you have any doubts about the best course of action, you should consult a qualified independent financial adviser. This chapter will help you choose an adviser, if you do not already have one, or if you are unhappy with the adviser you already have.

Independent financial adviser and *Moneywise* Ask the Professionals panellist Brian Dennehy says:

"You won't get many chances to get your retirement planning right. Test your independent financial adviser from the outset. As well as an in depth initial report, his or her service should include annual feedback and meetings. In this way you can continually monitor the initial advice and underlying assumptions, and make adjustments when needed. You can penny-pinch and forgo independent and professional advice, but don't be surprised if your retirement income suffers."

Not everyone needs a financial adviser; you can buy a pension direct from the provider instead. A few years ago this would have been almost impossible, but changes in the market mean that nowadays most large firms are willing to deal with you direct – some do not conduct their business any other way.

But remember that the advice an insurance company can give you is strictly limited – it will tell you only about its own products. Even if another company's product is more suitable for you, the insurance company is not allowed to tell you this.

In the past almost anyone could set up as a financial adviser, and many did. The Financial Services Act of 1986 made many changes to regulations which affected advisers and sales forces which sold investment products. The Financial Services Act 1986 applies only to policies and plans where your money is being used to fund an investment: pensions, savings plans and most (but not all) life insurance. It does not apply to motor or home insurance, or most types of medical insurance. All references to advisers in this chapter mean 'advisers who are selling investment plans'. The rules for non-investment plans are different, and are not covered here.

Since 1995, most advisers have been regulated by the Personal Investment Authority (PIA). As well as regulating most advisers, the PIA is responsible for many of the life insurance companies and since its inception a new and stricter regulatory regime is being introduced. The following are among the many changes which have taken effect since 1995:

○ Financial advisers now have to be qualified, and had until July 1997 to pass the necessary examinations; they also have on-going requirements for training and competence. The minimum qualification allowable is the Financial Planning Certificate (FPC) or its equivalents – the Certificate for Financial Advisers (CeFA) and the Investment Advice Certificate (IAC).
○ Customers must be told how much commission a financial adviser is being paid as a result of the purchase of an investment product.
○ Customers must also be supplied with a Key Features document (see Chapter 11).

Not all insurance companies have to belong to the PIA. They can choose instead to be regulated directly by the Financial Services Authority – the PIA's own regulator. Most financial advisers belong to the PIA, but non-IFA advisers must have certification from the recognised professional body (RPB). The RPBs are:

The Chartered Institute of Certified Accountants
The Institute of Actuaries
The Institute of Chartered Accountants in England and Wales
The Institute of Chartered Accountants in Scotland
The Institute of Chartered Accountants in Ireland
The Insurance Brokers Registration Council
The Law Society of England and Wales
The Law Society of Scotland
The Law Society of Northern Ireland.

The amount of income which members of these bodies can derive from the selling of investment products is limited.

Regulators such as the PIA have the power to reprimand and fine their members when they break the rules. In extreme cases, the member can be closed down and put out of business by the regulator.

Both types of adviser have a duty to give you 'best advice'. This means

Financial advisers fall into two categories:

○ Independent advisers, who are not associated with any one life insurance company. They can sell any product on the market, as long as it is the best one for you.

○ 'Tied agents', or company representatives, who are linked to one insurance company for investment business. They cannot sell the products of another insurance company. They can only sell you a suitable product from the range available to them from the insurance company to which they are linked. If they do not have a suitable product, they have a duty to tell you, and cannot simply sell you the next best thing on their list.

that they must take reasonable care to recommend the most suitable policy for you, given your circumstances, objectives and attitude to risk. Best advice does not mean that if you approached ten financial advisers, they would all recommend exactly the same policy to meet your needs. Investment policies after all depend on future performance, which is not guaranteed by looking at past performance, so inevitably there will be an element of subjective decision in a recommendation.

Best advice means that – in the case of the ten advisers – they would all recommend plans or policies which were very similar in the need which they met and in the level of risk attached to the investment.

Choosing an adviser – what should you ask?

First of all, where do you find out about financial advisers? You could look in the Yellow Pages, or in local business directories. It will not always be easy to tell from the entry in the directory whether the adviser is tied or independent.

If you contact Independent Financial Advice Promotion (IFAP), it will provide you free of charge with the details of three independent financial advisers in your area. Not all financial advisers are members of IFAP, however, so there is absolutely no guarantee that you will be given the names and addresses of the very best advisers operating in your area, but IFAP is a good place to start.

151

Checklist – questions to ask a financial adviser

○ Ask about a financial adviser's qualifications. The minimum qualification, as discussed on page 150, is the FPC or one of its equivalents. Many advisers also have additional qualifications, such as the Advanced Financial Planning Certificate (AFPC) or the Professional Investment Certificate (PIC), and the industry encourages them to obtain these. Advisers dealing with pension transfers must, from 1 April 1999, have passed a specialist exam. Ask to see proof of their qualifications.

○ Ask your adviser how long he or she has been in business.

○ Ask how many complaints have been received, as a proportion of the number of investment plans sold.

○ Ask about the firm. How many advisers does it have: too few and you could find yourself struggling to get advice if the adviser is ill or on holiday; too many, and there is a danger that the company is more interested in processing sales than in genuinely giving advice.

○ How many clients does your adviser have personally? Very few could make you doubt his or her competence; very many means that the adviser may not have the time to give you the attention you want.

○ Does your adviser have any pensions qualifications? Is he or she an Associate of the Pensions Management Institute (APMI).

○ What proportion of business comes from pensions? A very low percentage may mean that knowledge of pensions may be poor and out of date.

○ Ask the adviser to give you the names of other clients you can approach, to see what they think of this adviser. You can only expect the adviser to give you the names of clients who will respond favourably, but if the adviser is unwilling to give you any names, be cautious. You could also ask the adviser for the names of other professionals who have referred their clients to the adviser, such as other people's accountants and solicitors, then get in touch with those professionals and find out their opinions on the adviser.

If you have an accountant or solicitor, you can ask them for the names of any financial advisers whom they have worked with and whom they would be prepared to recommend. If you have an ongoing relationship with your accountant or solicitor, he or she will be unwilling to recommend to you an unsuitable or untrustworthy adviser, because if you are unhappy with the advice they give, they could, potentially, run the risk of losing you as a client.

Having contacted a financial adviser, you must satisfy yourself that you can trust this person, and would be comfortable to act on the advice you are given.

How the adviser is paid

Finally, ask the adviser how he or she is paid. Advisers either charge you a fee for their time, or they are paid by means of commission paid to them by the insurance company when they sell you a product.

Do not be fooled by the word 'commission' – it is not the insurance company's money which is being used to pay the commission. It is yours. Every penny of commission paid to a financial adviser comes out of the money you pay towards your insurance or pension plan.

With certain types of investment plans, including pensions, the adviser will be paid a sum of money equal to all your first year's contributions. This is often paid as a lump sum upfront, so all the money you pay at the start is going to pay off the adviser's commission. Very little – if any – of your contributions are going towards the investment you have just bought!

Although it may appear more costly in the short term, in the long term it can be far better to use the services of an adviser who charges fees for the services given, instead of taking commission. You will have a clear idea of what the fee-based advice is going to cost you, and the confidence that your monthly contributions are going into your pension plan. The Consumers' Association also found – in a recent report – that 'you are most likely to receive unbiased, detailed advice from an independent financial adviser who charges fees or at least gives the option of fees'.

Some advisers will tell you that they are fee-based, but that they offset their fees against the commission they receive, so you may not have to pay anything for the advice. If your adviser does this, be careful:

○ Commission is still being paid, so your contributions are still going to the adviser and not into your pension. You could be making a short-term saving at the expense of your investment.

○ Make sure that you receive a detailed statement of the cost of the advice given, offset against the commission received. If more commission is received than the cost of the fees, then you should be entitled to

153

that surplus commission – if the adviser truly is fee based.

If you decide to increase the level of contributions into your pension at some point in the future, those advisers who charge commission may well be paid commission on the increase – despite having nothing to do with this future decision. You can instruct the insurance company not to pay commission in these circumstances, but many advisers rely on the fact that clients are not generally aware of this practice.

What should a financial adviser ask you?

Once you have chosen a suitable financial adviser, you should expect to undergo a 'fact-find' with that adviser. This will be a very detailed examination of your financial situation.

The fact-find may not seem immediately relevant to the stated purpose of your appointment. However, in order to give you best advice, the adviser must know all the necessary information about you and your circumstances.

YOUR RISK PROFILE
One of the most essential aspects of personal financial planning is to be clear about your attitude to investment risk:

○ Are you no-risk or low-risk? The thought of losing any part of your investment worries you. You do not want to invest in anything which could result in your losing a part of your initial capital. You would prefer lower returns from your money if it means that you are secure in the knowledge that your money is safe.
○ Are you high-risk? You want to make the very most of your money, and that means you are prepared to risk your capital in investments where there is the possibility of losing part or most of it. You are happy to trade losses in the short and medium term for much greater gains in the long term.
○ Are you somewhere in between? You do not want to invest your money in high-risk areas, but you accept that you need to make more from your capital than merely placing it in high-interest deposit

What a fact-find should ask you and your partner

○ Your name, address, age and place of birth, marital status, health, and whether or not you are a smoker.

○ The number of children and other dependants that you have, how old they are and what is their state of health.

○ The names, ages, occupations and state of health of other immediate family members.

○ Your occupation, income (including bonuses and perks), and whether or not your employer offers medical insurance, life cover, and a pension scheme.

○ Your assets and liabilities, regular savings and regular outgoings.

○ What insurance and investments you already have.

○ What pension arrangements you already have.

○ Your current views on the level of insurance and investments which you have.

○ Finally, your attitude to risk.

accounts or gilts. Pooled investments such as PEPs and unit trusts will make more of your money, and you can choose to invest in markets which minimise the risk to your capital, while still producing healthy investment gains.

The fundamental consideration about any investment, whether it is your pension or other savings, is that you should not invest in schemes or markets which do not suit your risk profile, and you should not allow your financial adviser to sell you a policy or plan which does not match it.

The advice process

From the fact-find, your financial adviser should be able to form a comprehensive picture of your current situation and your objectives. He or she will then produce a report for you, which summarises your position.

It will contain much of the information you provided in the fact-find. Check this information to make sure it is correct – if it is not, this may suggest the adviser is not very thorough.

The adviser may propose different priorities from those you have outlined. This is not unusual.

What happens if the adviser identifies different priorities from the priorities you have outlined? First of all, you should listen carefully to the arguments put forward – your financial adviser is making these suggestions because they meet your needs. But the adviser cannot force you to follow the list of priorities he or she has identified. You cannot be made to buy anything which you do not want. If you disagree over priorities, the adviser has to draw up an agreed list of priorities with you. This should go into the revised report.

Once you have agreed on the priority need which has to be met, the adviser will then go on to recommend a particular plan to meet that need. Where an adviser is recommending a particular plan or policy to you, there has to be a short justification of why Company A's product has been chosen above all the others. It should briefly state the nature of the policy and its suitability to you as the client. The report should also compare Company A's policy against other similar policies on the market, especially in terms of investment performance.

By doing this, the adviser is demonstrating that Company A's policy has been chosen above all the others because it is among the best – not because Company A will pay higher commission to the adviser.

WHAT HAPPENS IF YOU ARE GIVEN BAD ADVICE?

First of all, what is bad advice? You have been given bad advice if you have been sold something which is not suitable for you, or advised to take a course of action which has harmed you financially. If you have been sold a life insurance policy when you already have life insurance cover through your employer, and your adviser knew this, then that would be bad advice. If you were a member of your employers pension scheme, to which your employer contributed, and you were advised to transfer out to a personal pension where your employer did not contribute, that would almost certainly be bad advice. There would have to be very good reasons for that transfer – and the adviser should have documented the reasons at the time.

But if you buy a pension plan or an endowment policy from Company A, and then you discover that Company B's pension plan or endowment has fared better through a more successful investment policy, that is unlikely to be bad advice. All advisers assess the policies on the market based on what they know of the company and its past performance. Past

Example
You are a man of 34 with a wife and two young children. You are self-employed, earning around £25,000 a year. Your wife works part-time, fitting it around caring for the children, and earns £6,000 a year. You want to start a pension, but in your circumstances the adviser is required to assess your other needs first. You do not have any life insurance – at your age, with a dependent wife and children, you should have a term insurance policy to protect them in case you die.

As a self-employed person, you should also have income replacement insurance (also known as permanent health insurance – PHI) to provide an income if you cannot work through illness or disability.

Under the procedures for giving best advice, an adviser must bring to your attention the fact that you have needs more urgent than starting a pension – in this case, taking out life and health insurance.

performance is no guarantee of future performance, and so the advisers use their knowledge and experience to evaluate which company will – in their opinion – perform well in the future.

As long as they have taken all reasonable steps to make that judgement fairly, then you have not been badly advised. You and your adviser have simply been unlucky that Company B has done better than forecast, and in the future, you may find that Company A starts to perform well again.

Only if your adviser did not assess the available policies and companies fairly could you argue that you were given bad advice. If there was no justification of Company A's policy against its competitors at the time of the sale, then that could be considered bad advice.

If you have reason to assume that you have been given bad advice, in the first case you should contact both the provider of your pension or other investment plan, and also your adviser. They should work with you to answer your complaint.

A financial adviser regulated by the PIA is obliged to report an investment complaint which has not been resolved after six months to that body. The PIA will take an active interest in the case from then on. If your adviser or pension provider does not answer your complaint to your satisfaction, you can complain directly to the adviser's regulator – usually the PIA.

If your complaint relates to the administration of your pension, you can complain to the Occupational Pensions Advisory Service, which gives advice free of charge to people having trouble with both personal and employers pensions. As a final resort, if you still believe you have a legitimate complaint which has to be answered, you can contact the Pensions Ombudsman.

If you lose money as a result of the adviser's firm going out of business – for example if the adviser was holding funds on your behalf – then you can make a claim against the Investors' Compensation Scheme. You would be able to claim for a substantial part of your loss – all of the first £30,000 and 90% of the next £20,000 lost.

Addresses for these bodies can be found in the Directory at the end of the book.

Bear in mind that changes to regulation are ongoing. In 1998, the Financial Services Authority (FSA) was created to take over the responsibilities of the former regulator, the Securities and Investments Board. By 1999,

Independent financial adviser and *Moneywise* Ask the Professionals panellist Kean Seager says:

"The concept of 'bad advice' really is a difficult grey area and it is particularly difficult for the layperson to assess. If you feel you have been given poor advice it is probably best to ask an independent expert for an opinion."

Who can help me with my pension query?

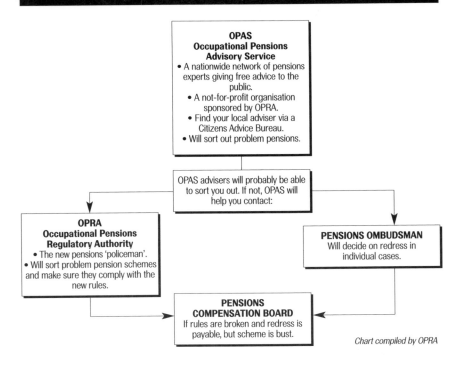

OPAS
Occupational Pensions Advisory Service
• A nationwide network of pensions experts giving free advice to the public.
• A not-for-profit organisation sponsored by OPRA.
• Find your local adviser via a Citizens Advice Bureau.
• Will sort out problem pensions.

OPAS advisers will probably be able to sort you out. If not, OPAS will help you contact:

OPRA
Occupational Pensions Regulatory Authority
• The new pensions 'policeman'.
• Will sort problem pension schemes and make sure they comply with the new rules.

PENSIONS OMBUDSMAN
Will decide on redress in individual cases.

PENSIONS COMPENSATION BOARD
If rules are broken and redress is payable, but scheme is bust.

Chart compiled by OPRA

the FSA is due to have absorbed the other financial services regulators, including the PIA and to have taken over the investment responsibilities of other regulators, such as the Bank of England. A new Financial Services Act is due to broaden the scope of financial regulation.

Action plan

○ If you are choosing a new financial adviser, make sure that you check his or her credentials thoroughly. Ask to see qualifications, and ask to speak to other clients, or professionals such as solicitors with whom the adviser works.

○ Be clear about your objectives before you see the adviser. Prepare yourself by listing the information you will be asked in the fact-find (see page 155).

○ Decide your attitude to risk before you see an adviser.

○ If you are doubtful about the advice given, do not buy the pension or investment plan being offered.

○ If you think you have been given bad advice, complain first of all to your adviser; second, to the regulator and, finally, to the Pensions Ombudsman if necessary.

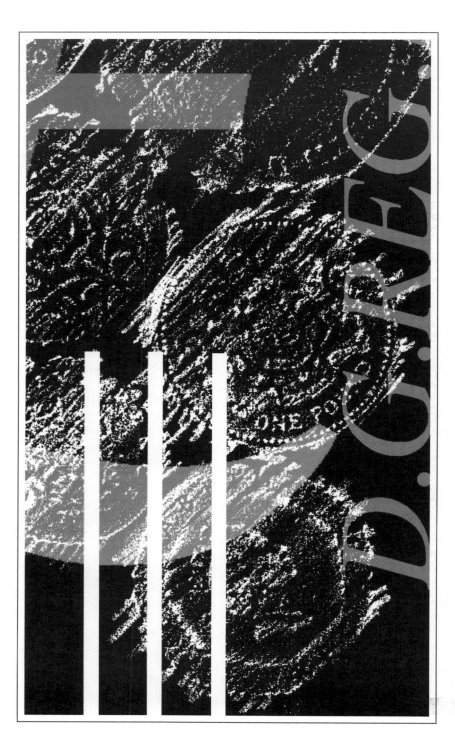

13 Checking your pension's progress

You have made your decision – you are a member of your employer's pension scheme, or you have taken out your personal pension and are contributing to it as planned. But what happens now – do you simply put the whole thing out of your mind until the time comes for you to retire?

It is important to check on your pension, whatever type of scheme you are in. If you are in an employers scheme, the rules allow you to top up your pension. This is explained in Chapter 14. Whatever type of scheme you are in, you might also want to use certain types of investment to build up an extra fund to provide income in retirement (see Chapter 15).

Independent financial adviser and *Moneywise* Ask the Professionals panellist Rebekah Kearey says:

"Nothing stays the same for long and pension planning should be reviewed as frequently as income or other circumstances change. To discover a pension is inadequate when you're 65 and three-quarters is very shocking indeed."

State pensions

To find out the forecast value of your basic state pension and your SERPS pension if you are contracted in to SERPS, pick up a form BR19 'Request for a Retirement Pension Forecast' from your local Benefits Agency office.

Send it to the DSS, which will provide you with a forecast of what you can expect from the State. This will be based on your working record to date, and will make assumptions about your work in the future, assuming that you continue working until your state retirement age.

If there are gaps in your National Insurance contributions record, you may not be entitled to the maximum State pension. Certain gaps in contributions can be made up by credits from the DSS, if you were not working or contributing (see Chapter 4).

If you have gaps in your record which cannot be closed by DSS credits, then you can elect to make voluntary National Insurance contributions. You can do this by making Class 3 contributions to the DSS. The current rate for Class 3 contributions is £6.25 a week (see Chapter 4).

To find out more, obtain a copy of the leaflet CA08 'National Insurance voluntary contributions' from your local Benefits Agency office.

Employers schemes

FINAL SALARY SCHEMES

Members of final salary company schemes are in the best position to check on their pension's progress. Because the scheme promises to pay a proportion of the final salary for each year of membership of the scheme, it is relatively easy to predict what your pension will be. If you stay in the scheme for the full period, then you will be entitled to the maximum pension under the scheme's rules.

Each year that you are an employee, your scheme's administrator will send you a statement of your pension's progress. This will contain:

○ An outline of the retirement benefit you can expect at normal scheme retirement age if you stay in the scheme.
○ The maximum lump sum to which you would be entitled.
○ The reduced pension you could have if you took the maximum lump sum.
○ The pension(s) payable to your survivors.
○ The life insurance benefit your survivors could receive if you die in service, if the scheme offers this.

All figures will be given in terms of your current salary, so it gives you an indication of your pension in today's values. Since most people can assume that their salary will increase at least in line with inflation, this is a useful indicator of the standard of living you can expect from your pension.

Remember that this is a forecast – if you leave the scheme or retire earlier than the normal scheme retirement date, the pension you will receive will be less than the projection which is made today.

If you are in a final salary scheme and know that you will not reach the maximum benefits under the scheme, you should consider topping up your pension. This can be done either by paying AVCs or free-standing additional voluntary contributions (FSAVCs) (see Chapter 14).

The scheme's investments
A final salary scheme promises to pay you the benefits associated with your salary and length of service. If the scheme's investments underperform, the employer has to make up any difference, especially under the new minimum funding requirements introduced by the 1995 Pensions Act (see Chapter 6). But if the scheme does underperform, it could still have implications for your pension. The employer may not be able to afford planned enhancements to the scheme, so future improvements in your pension may not happen.

Most final salary schemes plan to increase the pensions being paid out to pensioners to make sure that their spending power is not eroded. The scheme is obliged to pay increases on parts of the pension (see Chapter 5). But a major part of the pension is entitled only to discretionary increases, so if the scheme underperforms badly, the trustees of the scheme may be put under pressure by the employer not to make cost-of-living increases. In extreme cases, the employer may decide to end the scheme altogether.

Schemes have to supply an annual report; most publish it to the members in a more user-friendly version. Make sure that you obtain a copy of this each year and look at the section covering the investment performance of the pension fund. Find out what the targets set for the fund managers are, and see if they have been met. Most companies participate in schemes which analyse and compare all pension schemes so you can see how your pension fund is performing against other similar funds.

Most trustees set targets for their pension fund managers against the average performance of the schemes with which they are compared. Fund managers may have to perform above average, or within 1% each way of the average. It should be possible to tell from the annual report whether the fund managers have reached their target. If they have not, contact your staff pensions representative or member-nominated trustee and have them raise the issue in the next trustees' meeting. After all, the fund managers are working for the trustees, who have a duty towards you as a member. If the fund managers aren't doing their jobs, the trustees should be doing something about it.

If the pension fund overperforms – the assets of the scheme are greater than its liabilities – you should also be aware of this. The question of who owns the surplus is still complex and unclear. Most schemes operate on the principle that if an employer wishes to take the surplus from a pension scheme, the following should occur:

○ The surplus should first be used to increase pensions currently being paid to pensioners.
○ Next it should be used to enhance the benefits of the scheme to all members.
○ Finally, any remaining surplus can be taken by the employer.

It is worth being aware of a surplus – if it exists. And you can always ask your trustee representatives to press for enhancements to the scheme.

MONEY PURCHASE SCHEMES

In a money purchase scheme your final pension depends entirely on the underlying performance of the assets invested on your behalf. There is no guaranteed pension when you retire. Targeted money purchase schemes are slightly different, though even in this case there is no guaranteed sum (see Chapter 7).

Each year your pension scheme will supply a statement of your projected position that will be based on contributions and investment performance to date. Assumptions are made about the future level of contributions, and also about future investment growth. You should be aware that the growth assumptions used are examples only. The actual investment performance may be very different.

The annual statement shows the assumed pension you would be able to buy with the projected fund. Again, this is not guaranteed – the actual pension you can buy with the fund will depend on annuity rates when you retire, and the features you want from your annuity.

Members of money purchase schemes are vulnerable to the fluctuations of the investment market. It is therefore much more important for you to be aware of the pension fund's performance than if you were in a final salary scheme.

Your course of action is similar to that of a member of a final salary scheme. Make sure that you obtain the annual report each year and study it closely to see if the fund managers are performing according to their targets. If they are not, speak to your trustee representative. You should ensure that the question is raised at the next trustees' meeting, so that the fund managers have to justify their actions.

Many money purchase schemes operate on the basis of a number of funds, covering the range of investment risk. Schemes invest the contributions on behalf of a member according to his or her age and impending retirement date:

○ When you are young and retirement is a long way off, the contributions made on your behalf may be invested in high-yielding funds where there is the possibility of short-term loss. This will, however, be offset by the potential of much larger long-term gains.

○ As you approach retirement, the scheme will start to shift contributions and the assets accumulated in your name into lower-risk funds where gains are more modest. This approach avoids you suffering a reverse in your pension fund just before retirement.

If you are in this type of scheme, you can take a more active role in deciding the fund in which your assets are invested, rather than just leaving the decisions to the pension fund managers.

Independent financial adviser and *Moneywise* Ask the Professionals panellist Brian Dennehy says:

"The understanding of risk decreases the higher the stockmarket rises – and that includes both the general public and those within the investment industry. If you understand this and have the time, why not get involved with your own investments?"

If you don't belong to this type of scheme, you could ask the trustees if you can make your own investments. This is likely to appeal only to higher-paid individuals, perhaps earning over £100,000 a year. The trustees can set up a separate scheme for your contributions only. You select a fund manager to handle your fund, and ask the trustees to appoint that manager. But your own pension fund will have to bear the costs of the fund manager's time, and of the related administration. In many ways this approach is similar to having a personal pension, but still within your company scheme, and allowing you the benefit of your employer's contributions.

Personal pensions

Each year your pension provider will send you a statement similar in content to that supplied to members of money purchase company schemes. Based on contributions and investment performance to date, the statement makes assumptions about future contributions and future investment growth. The assumptions used are examples only. The actual investment performance may be very different.

The statement will also show the forecast pension you would be able to buy with the projected fund. Again, this is not guaranteed – the actual pension you can buy will depend on annuity rates when you retire, and the features you want from your pension.

To track the performance of your pension provider against others in its sector, you may need to resort to magazines such as *Money Management*, *Planned Savings* and *Pensions Management Monthly*, which publish league tables and regular surveys of personal pensions. The magazines are designed for financial advisers, and so you may find them difficult to understand without help, but once your financial adviser has explained what to look for you should be able to refer to them only once a year or so.

If you are unhappy about the performance of the provider, it is important to take the long-term view. All fund managers have bad years – only worry if your provider consistently underperforms. In fact, if your provider has a bad year, it is likely to shake up its fund management teams to improve performance in the future in order to attract new business. So a bad year or two may make your pension provider more attractive in subsequent years, as it strives to get back to the top of the league tables. But it can be a good idea to get in touch with your pension provider for an explanation.

If your personal pension has the option of more than one fund in which to be invested, you can move from a cautious fund into one offering the potential of higher yields. Again, be careful: do not invest in funds unless you are happy with the level of risk. As a general rule, you should stick to safe funds in the last ten years before retirement to secure modest investment gains rather than risk losing a significant portion of your fund in the months before you retire.

Schemes that have more than one fund will normally allow you to make one switch between funds each year, free of charge. Additional switches in a year can usually be made at a fairly modest cost. Again, be wary of switching funds simply because the fund in which you have invested has had a poor year.

As a final resort, if you remain unhappy with your personal pension scheme, you can consider moving to another provider. There are costs associated with this, but it may be worth it if in the long term you benefit from a larger pension fund.If you move to another pension provider, you can either leave your pension assets behind in the existing pension scheme, or transfer them to your new provider. Transferring will incur penalties, but at least the assets transferred will benefit from the new provider's investment policies. If you freeze your assets, they remain under the existing investment strategy, which you have decided to leave, and you will have to pay management charges to the old and new provider.

Action plan

○ Whatever type of pension you have, you should expect a statement of your personal benefits each year. You will not receive one for a preserved pension unless you ask. Read it carefully, and query anything you do not understand with your pension scheme administrator or pension provider.

○ If you are a member of a final salary company scheme, your pension benefits are guaranteed, but you should take an interest in the investment success of the scheme's assets.

○ If you have a personal pension, or are a member of a money purchase company scheme, it is very important that you monitor your pension fund's investment performance – the pension you receive when you retire will entirely depend on this. Where possible, take a more active role in deciding the funds into which your assets are invested. If you are in a money purchase scheme, you should lobby the trustees in the same way as a member of a final salary scheme, in order to get better performance from the fund managers.

○ Whatever scheme you belong to, remember to take the long-term view. All investments have bad periods from time to time, and it is the longer-term performance that really matters.

If you are concerned about the progress of your pension, and are uncertain about the best course of action to take, then consult a qualified independent financial adviser.

14 Topping up your pension

There are a number of reasons why you may wish to top up your pension scheme, and, fortunately, there are also various ways of boosting your pension arrangements – all of them within Inland Revenue limits.

If you are in an employers pension scheme, the maximum pension you can retire on under Inland Revenue rules is two-thirds of your final salary. But in practice few people would achieve this maximum pension simply by making their normal contributions to their pension scheme. If you are not one of those lucky few, you should consider ways of topping up your pension.

Independent financial adviser and *Moneywise* Ask the Professionals panellist Kean Seager says:

"These days many people retire early and life expectancy is increasing all the time. It is not unusual for people to have as long in retirement as they did in work. So it is important that you top up your pension if you possibly can. Retirement is for enjoying and it is going to take a certain amount of money to enable you to do just that."

If you have a personal pension, there is no limit to the pension you can retire on. But if you are self-employed, you may have experienced periods when you were unable to contribute to your pension. Again you may need to top it up.

WHY SHOULD I TOP UP MY PENSION?

○ If you joined your company scheme late, or if you have moved jobs a number of times, or have taken a career break (to raise children for example), your normal contributions will not allow you to reach the maximum pension.

○ Your company scheme may accrue at an unfavourable rate. If it accrues at lower that 1/60, then you would not be able to reach the maximum two-thirds pension by the time you retire. A top-up would therefore help to improve your position.

169

○ Your company scheme may not include all your earnings in assessing the level of pension it will pay, for example ignoring overtime and bonuses.

○ It may disregard part of your salary – roughly the first £3,000 a year – because it assumes you will be entitled to the basic state pension.

○ It may not include important benefits such as a company car in assessing your final salary.

○ If you are self-employed, there may have been years when you made no contribution to your pension, or only a small one.

How you go about topping up, and the limits on what you can contribute to your pension, differ between employers pension schemes and personal pensions.

Employers pension schemes

Maximum contributions If you are in an employers pension scheme, the maximum you can contribute in any year will be 15% of your total earnings. As discussed earlier (see Chapter 5), this is not just your salary – you can include all taxable benefits in calculating your total earnings.

In most employers pension schemes, employees contribute 5% to 6% of their salary. You would therefore have the scope to contribute another 9% to 10% of your salary to a top-up scheme.

If you are a post-89 member, then the earnings cap applies to your pension contributions (see Chapter 5). The earnings cap is currently set at £87,600 (1998/99). If you earn above that limit, you can only contribute 15% of the £87,600.

TOPPING UP YOUR OCCUPATIONAL PENSION

Members of employers pension schemes can top up their pensions by making AVCs. These can either be in association with your employer's pension scheme, or you can buy

Example
You are a man earning £30,000 a year. You have a company car, and your employer provides you with medical insurance. You pay tax on both of these benefits.

Salary	£30,000
Company car (taxable value)	£3,500
Medical insurance	£400
Total earnings for calculating pension contributions	£33,900

AVCs or FSAVCs – which should I choose?

○ Employers' in-house AVCs are linked to your main scheme. If you change jobs, you stop paying into the AVCs at the same time that you stop paying into your main pension scheme. If you preserve your main pension scheme, the AVCs are also preserved. FSAVCs on the other hand can be continued when you join your new employer's scheme.

○ Your company's pension scheme may have a cautious investment policy. FSAVCs could provide better returns for the same money. But remember, if you do not like risking your money, the cautious approach may be the best one for you. And the closer you are to retirement, the more cautious you should be with your investments.

○ The charges on FSAVCs will probably be higher than those on in-house AVCs, where your employer will bear part of the costs.

free-standing AVCs (FSAVCs) from a different pension provider such as an insurance company, bank or building society.

If you contribute to your employer's in-house AVCs, then the extra benefits may be in the form of additional years (if you are in a final salary scheme) or in the form of an additional fund on retirement (if you are in a money purchase scheme). Benefits will be linked to the main scheme – so you cannot specify an earlier retirement date for your AVCs. FSAVCs must also be taken out with the same retirement date as your employers scheme. FSAVCs always operate on a money purchase basis, and will build up in a fund completely separate from your main pension fund.

The Inland Revenue limits – a maximum contribution of 15% of gross salary a year, and a maximum pension of two-thirds final salary – apply to the combined main scheme pension and AVCs or FSAVCs. For in-house AVCs the checks are straightforward and are the responsibility of the scheme administrators, who have to ensure that the contributions do not exceed the limit, and that the projected benefits will remain within the maximum of two-thirds final salary. The scheme administrators will limit the amount you contribute to prevent you overfunding your pension.

If you have FSAVCs, you need to check two things:

○ First, the provider has to obtain information from your employer in order to check your estimated gross salary for the year. This information is combined with the proposed contributions to the FSAVCs, to

AVC calculator

Use this calculator to work out how much you can pay in AVCs

£ a year

Your earnings   A
Include salary, commission, bonuses,
overtime payments, the taxable value of
fringe benefits.

Earnings cap   B
If the post-1989 rules apply, enter the
lower of your earnings or £87,600.

The most you can contribute   C
Multiply **A** or **B** by 15 and divide by 100.

Your current contributions   D
Enter the amount you are paying each
year in contributions – your payslips or
form P60 will tell you this.

How much you can pay in AVCs   E
Subtract **D** from **C** – what is left is the
amount you can pay in AVCs to top
up your pension.

ensure you are not contributing more than you are allowed.

○ Second, there is the 'headroom check' to make sure that the pension itself will not exceed the two-thirds final salary limit:

• if you are contributing more than £2,400 a year to the FSAVCs, the company providing the FSAVCs must check that your total contributions – to both your main occupational pension and the FSAVCs – will not take your projected pension over the maximum two-thirds final salary limit. This is referred to as a 'headroom check'.

• if your contributions to the FSAVCs are less than £2,400 a year, the headroom check will only be made upon retirement. If you have over-funded your pension at that point, the surplus will be refunded (minus tax, currently at a rate of 33% for basic-rate taxpayers and 46% for higher-rate taxpayers).

If you are a post-89 member, the earnings cap applies to both AVCs and FSAVCs – you can only contribute a maximum of 15% of salary, up to the limit of £87,600 (1998/99). In addition, if your final salary is larger than the earnings cap limit, your pension cannot be greater than two-thirds of the earnings cap.

When you retire, the benefits from your additional contributions are added to your main scheme. You can take all the benefits as a pension, or you can take the option of a tax-free lump sum, up to a maximum of 1·5 times final salary. However, in most cases the lump sum can only be taken from your main scheme benefits. FSAVCs, and most AVCs, can only be taken as pension. The exceptions are AVCs held by pre-87 members, who can take a tax-free lump sum from their AVCs.

In practice, you can take the same size of lump sum whatever regime you are under – if you cannot take it from the AVCs, you take it from the main scheme, and use the AVCs pension to compensate for the main scheme pension you have lost by taking the lump sum. The only problem is that your main scheme pension will usually benefit from increases which will not be available to the AVCs pension. So if your pension from the main scheme is smaller than it might have been – because you took more as a lump sum – the proportion of your pension which increases each year will also be smaller.

Personal pensions

Maximum contributions If you have a personal pension, the limits on contributions depend on your age and net relevant earnings (see Chapter 10), which are your income minus all business expenses, business losses, or capital allowances.

You cannot make a contribution to your pension if you do not have net relevant earnings.

The age limits are a stepped scale, as shown in Chapter 10, and are designed to allow people to make larger contributions as they get older and have less time to build their pension. The earnings cap of £87,600 (1998/99) applies to all personal pension plans. If you have net relevant earnings over this sum of money, you cannot include them in your calculation to work out your maximum pension contribution.

Topping up a personal pension

If you have a personal pension, you cannot buy AVCs or FSAVCs. Instead, you have a series of allowances called carry forward and carry back, which allow you to maximise the contributions you make by using any left-over contribution allowances from previous tax years.

Carry forward means that if you have not made the maximum contribution allowed in any of the previous six tax years, you are allowed to make pension contributions against those allowances. You have to use all of your current year's allowance first. If you have surplus money to make contributions after that, you must use the oldest years' allowances first.

You can therefore make a far greater contribution to your pension than you could if you were only able to use your current year's allowance. If you have had a few lean years of trading as a self-employed person, carry forward is an efficient way of making up for the pension contributions you may have missed in the past.

To take advantage of carry forward relief, you should complete Inland Revenue forms PP42 and PP120.

Carry back means that you can use up any unused allowance from the previous tax year only. You can elect to have the payment treated as if it applies to that tax year, which is useful if you were a higher-rate taxpayer in the previous year, but will not be one in the current year. The pension contribution carried back to the previous year will be given tax relief at the higher rate. Or, you can delay making a pension contribution in one year – to help your cash flow, for example – and still gain the tax reliefs for that year.

> **Example**
> You have a personal pension to which you have not contributed in the last four years. You now have a cash surplus, and wish to contribute to your pension. Under carry forward, you have to start with the unused allowance from four years ago. Next, you use up the allowance from three years ago, and so on.
>
> But last year, you were a higher-rate taxpayer, and you want to get the maximum tax relief from your contributions. Carry back allows you to make a contribution for last year, regardless of whether or not you have unused allowances in earlier years. Paying your contribution under carry back allows you to use up last year's allowance, and get the higher rate of tax relief.

Example

A man aged 38 has net relevant earnings of £25,000 for the 1998/99 tax year. In addition he inherited £10,000 which he wishes to contribute to his personal pension. He can contribute in the 1998/99 tax year as follows:

Tax year	Age	Net relevant earnings	Contribution limit %	Maximum allowable contribution	Actual contribution	Unused allowance
98/99	38	£25,000	20%	£5,000	£5,000	£0

He still has £5,000 from his inheritance which he can contribute to his pension. Under carry forward rules, he can look at the six previous years. During these years he had relatively little spare cash, and could not make the maximum allowed contribution in any of those years.

Tax year	Age	Net relevant earnings	Contribution limit %	Maximum allowable contribution	Actual contribution	Unused allowance
92/93	32	£16,000	17.5%	£2,800	£1,500	£1,300
93/94	33	£17,500	17·5%	£3,062·50	£1,800	£1,262·50
94/95	34	£18,000	17·5%	£3,150	£1,500	£1,650
95/96	35	£20,000	17·5%	£3,500	£2,000	£1,500
96/97	36	£20,000	20%	£4,000	£2,200	£1,800
97/98	37	£22,000	20%	£4,400	£2,500	£1,900

He can therefore contribute £5,000 to his pension, using his spare allowances as follows:

	Available allowance	Contribution
92/93	£1,300·00	£1,300·00
93/94	£1,262·50	£1,262·50
94/95	£1,650·00	£1,650·00
95/96	£1,500·00	£787·50
96/97	£1,800·00	–
97/98	£1,900·00	–

Next year, if he again has money to invest over and above his 1999/2000 allowance, he still has £712·50 of his 1995/96 allowance to use, as well as £3,700 from his 1996/97 and 1997/98 allowances.

TOPPING UP YOUR PERSONAL PENSION CALCULATOR

Use this calculator to establish how much unused pensions tax relief you have available

| | A | | B | C | | D | |
Tax year	Net relevant earnings £	Age	Contribution limit % (from table on page 117)	Maximum contri-bution (AxB)	Actual contri-bution	Unused allowance (C-D)
92/93						
93/94						
94/95						
95/96						
96/97						
97/98						

A carry forward payment would have the same effect, but the difference is that with carry forward you have to start with the oldest years' unused allowances first. So you can only make a carry forward payment for last year if you have used up all the earlier allowances – and you may not have that much money to contribute.

With carry back, you can elect to pay a contribution against the previous tax year's allowance without using up any allowances from older years. To take advantage of carry back, you should complete Inland Revenue forms PP43 and PP120. It is possible to combine carry forward and carry back when contributing to your pension – this way, you can benefit from the most recent year first of all, and then direct surplus funds into the older years as well. This is useful if:

○ In your carry back year you had earnings which made you a higher-rate taxpayer, and you were only a basic-rate taxpayer in older years.
○ In your carry back year you have reached an age at which you are enti-tled to pay a larger proportion of your net relevant earnings into your pension.

In both these cases, you will get greater benefit from the carry back option than from the carry forward option, so if you have sufficient surplus cash, choose the carry back option first, and then carry forward with any remaining pension contributions.

Action plan

○ First of all, whichever type of pension you have, go back to the Retirement calculator in Chapter 2, and – if you haven't already done so – complete it so that you know what income you will need in retirement. This will give you something to compare your projected pension against.

○ If you are in an employers pension scheme, check the rules to see how it defines final salary. If this definition means that your maximum pension will be considerably less than two-thirds of your actual annual income (including bonuses, the benefit of having a company car, and so on), your lifestyle in retirement could be affected. You should therefore consider topping up your pension.

○ If you are in an employers pension and you know that you will not complete the years service needed for the maximum pension, consider topping up.

○ If you have a personal pension and have not contributed the maximum amount each year, make sure that you make contributions through carry forward and carry back whenever you have the spare cash to do so.

15 Other ways to save for your retirement

If you are one of the lucky few who will retire on the maximum pension allowed by the Inland Revenue, you should still consider other ways of boosting your income in retirement.

After all, that maximum pension is still only two-thirds of the income you have been used to. If it will be a struggle to achieve your desired lifestyle in retirement on your pension, you should look at other forms of investment. And if you are affected by the earnings cap, then your pension could be considerably less than two-thirds of the income you are used to. Remember, the earnings cap is not something that only high-fliers need to worry about. It may seem high today (£87,600 in 1998/99), but eventually, it could affect us all:

○ The earnings cap is increased in line with RPI – not with the generally faster-moving increases in average national earnings. So as each year passes, most people will find the gap between their income and the earnings cap narrowing.

○ The earnings cap does not have to be increased each year; it was not increased in 1993/94. As future chancellors try to reduce public spending, it could be squeezed again – after all, limiting the earnings cap limits the volume of pension contributions, which in turn limits the amount of tax the Inland Revenue misses out on.

Independent financial adviser and *Moneywise* Ask the Professionals panellist Brian Dennehy says:

"Tax is just one angle to consider in your retirement income planning. Pension plans are attractive because you get tax relief on the initial contribution. Personal Equity Plans (PEPs), for example, don't offer this, but do currently generate a tax-free income through retirement, and are far more flexible – it is these two features that mean you must strike a balance in your planning, not just relying on pension plans."

If you are hoping to retire early then you will need to make sure you have other arrangements in place. This chapter is also important if you do not have a pension because you cannot take one out. If you do not have any earnings, you cannot have a pension. So if you're planning to live off your capital, so you should be looking at the best ways to grow that capital and boost your retirement funds.

A range of options exists to meet the needs of people who want to invest money other than in approved pension schemes. Everyone needs to have a balanced range of savings and investments. There are three groups: cash-based, fixed interest and stockmarket-linked. By combining these types in suitable proportions you'll have a balanced portfolio. To build up capital to provide income in retirement, you need to look for growth investments. As you are investing for the long term, you can look at stockmarket investments. This means investing in shares, unit trusts or investment trusts. For the first-time stockmarket investor, unit trust or investment trusts are probably most suitable – your money is pooled with other investors' and spread across a range of investments. As explained in Chapter 11, you can invest across a range of markets through these funds: from risky emerging markets to staeady UK growth companies.

> Tax expert and *Moneywise* Ask the Professionals panellist Jane Adam says:
>
> "Despite the changes on the horizon, PEPs continue to provide tax advantages, particularly to higher-rate taxpayers who already use up their capital gains tax allowance."

Tax-free growth

It's also a good idea to make as much of that growth tax free.

PERSONAL EQUITY PLANS (PEPS)
To get a tax-free return on stockmarket investments you need to take out a PEP. You can hold shares, unit trusts, investment trusts and corporate bonds within a PEP. However, there are limits on how much you can invest:

○ £6,000 each year into a 'general' PEP: this is a PEP investing in a wide range of shares or funds.
○ £3,000 each year into a 'single company' PEP, which invests only in one company's shares.

Usually you have to pay tax of 20% on stockmarket income – dividends from shares or distributions from unit trusts. And there can be capital gains tax to pay when you sell stockmarket investments if you make a gain (there is a tax-free amount of £6,500 for the 1997/98 tax year). When your investments are in a PEP, you don't have to pay income tax on any income from these investments and you don't have to pay capital gains tax on any increase in value.

PEPs are not subject to any fixed timescale, unlike a pension or a Tax-Exempt Special Savings Account (TESSA) (see below). You can cash your PEP in and take the benefits at any time you like, which means it is an extremely flexible investment.

How risky your PEP is depends on the investments you hold in it. PEPs range from those investing in low-risk shares, where a lower rate of return is compensated for by increased security, to those investing in high-risk shares in return for potentially higher gains. So even though there is no minimum investment period for a PEP, you should consider a PEP to be a medium-term investment over three to five years. Holding a PEP for too short a period of time will expose you to the risk of short-term stockmarket losses.

PEP managers will charge an initial fee for setting up the PEP, and then an annual management charge of 1 to 2% of the fund.

You are allowed both types of PEP, so the maximum you could invest each year would be £9,000. If you invest in PEPs each year, then you can build up a substantial investment to supplement your pension in retirement.

From 6 April 1999, PEPs are being replaced by Individual Savings Accounts (ISAs) – see page 182. From that date, you will no longer be able to take out new PEPs but existing PEPs can continue for the time being. The government has said that for five years – ie until 5 April 2004 – the return on PEPs will continue to be tax-free, but be prepared for the tax breaks to be lost after that.

TAX-EXEMPT SPECIAL SAVINGS ACCOUNTS (TESSAs)

TESSAs are deposit accounts that benefit from special tax concessions. You have to invest in a TESSA for five years, and the maximum investment is £9,000 over the period.

If you are starting a new TESSA, you are limited to a maximum investment of £3,000 in the first year, and £1,800 in each of the following years. If you have made the maximum contributions in the first four years you can only contribute £600 in year five. If you have a maturing TESSA, you can roll-over the £9,000 capital from the mature TESSA (but not the interest) into a new TESSA.

If you hold a TESSA for five years according to the rules, all the interest payable is free of tax. If you make a withdrawal of capital, you will lose the tax-free status, and all the interest accruing will be liable for income tax. You can remove some of the proceeds from your TESSA without losing the tax-free benefits, but only that part of the interest each year which would be equivalent to the interest earned net of the tax relief.

Because you have to keep a TESSA for five years, and because you can only have one TESSA at a time, this is not a vehicle for significantly boosting your retirement savings. However, it provides a useful tax-free savings account, and can be a means of switching your investments from share-based products into deposit-based accounts in the years approaching retirement, a time when you should be reducing your exposure to the risks associated with share-based investments.

From 6 April 1999, TESSAs are due to be replaced by ISAs – see below. From that date, you can no longer start a new TESSA, but you can continue to contribute to an existing TESSA. If you have a TESSA which matures after 5 April 1999, you can reinvest the capital (but not the accumulated interest) in an ISA without it counting towards the ISA annual limits.

INDIVIDUAL SAVINGS ACCOUNTS (ISAS)

ISAs are being introduced from 6 April 1999 as the main form of tax-free savings for UK investors. You can use them to hold cash (ie bank accounts and National Savings products), life insurance and stocks and shares (including pooled investments such as unit trusts). The return from these will be completely tax-free.

There are limits on the amount you can put into your ISA each year. For 1999/2000 only, there is an overall limit of £7,000 with a maximum £3,000 for the cash element and £1,000 for life insurance. In subsequent years, the limits are £5,000 overall with a maximum £1,000 in cash and

£1,000 in life insurance.

You can choose to have one ISA each year invest-ing in some or all of the three elements. Alternatively, you can have up to three ISAs with each one investing in a different element – ie one for cash, one for life insurance and one for shares. In the latter case, there will be a limit of £3,000 a year on the amount invested in stocks and shares, whereas with a single ISA you can opt to invest the whole £7,000 (£5,000 in later years) in stocks and shares if you want to.

Under the tax rules, you can withdraw your money from an ISA at any time without losing the tax benefits. Like PEPs, ISAs will be run by plan managers who are free to set their own conditions and, of course, charges.

The ISA scheme will initially run for ten years. From the seventh year, it will be reviewed to decide what changes, if any, should be made once the ten years are up.

The amount you can invest in ISAs is substantially lower than the com-bined amounts you can currently invest in PEPs and TESSAs but, from 1999 onwards, ISAs will be the main alternative to consider if you are looking for tax-efficient non-pension investments.

When you retire

You can choose to leave your capital either in the investments them-selves, or in high-interest deposit accounts. TESSAs will lose their tax-free status when they mature, so you should think about moving the capital to an account offering better interest. (From April 1999 onwards, reinvest through an ISA).

Taking the proceeds from a maturing TESSA, a PEP or an ISA is tax free. With direct investment in unit trusts and investment trusts, you may be liable to income tax and capital gains tax. The proceeds of unit trusts or investment trusts will be assessed with the rest of your income and capital gains to calculate any liability.

Alternatively, you can use the proceeds from these investments to buy an additional annuity alongside your main pension scheme annuity. This type of annuity is known as a 'purchased life annuity', as opposed to the annuity bought with an approved pension scheme, called a 'scheme' or 'compulsory' annuity. A purchased life annuity is treated slightly more favourably for tax purposes:

○ You buy the annuity with the capital you have accumulated. Part of the income from the annuity is considered by the Inland Revenue to be the return of your capital – this part of the income is tax free.
○ The remaining income is treated as taxable in the normal way.

All of the income from the compulsory annuity bought with the proceeds of your pension scheme is subject to tax.

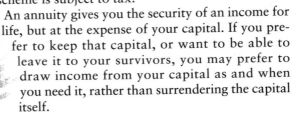

An annuity gives you the security of an income for life, but at the expense of your capital. If you prefer to keep that capital, or want to be able to leave it to your survivors, you may prefer to draw income from your capital as and when you need it, rather than surrendering the capital itself.

Action plan

For most people, the most tax-efficient way to invest for retirement is to make sure that their pension scheme is on course to deliver the maximum benefits. If you wish to make additional investments:

○ First of all, make sure that you are using your PEP allowance and, from April 1999, your ISA allowance, to the maximum. Invest in a general PEP rather than a single company PEP if you are cautious about stock-market investments.

○ Additional funds can be invested in unit trusts or investment trusts, but be aware of the potential tax liabilities when you take the proceeds. Consider cashing these investments in over a period of years, to obtain the full benefit of your personal capital gains tax allowance each year.

○ Make sure that you only choose investments that match your 'risk profile'.

○ If your employer is willing to make additional contributions to your pension, discuss the possibility of joining an unapproved pension scheme, either funded or unfunded.

○ As you approach retirement, switch your investments away from equity-based investments (PEPs, unit trusts, investment trusts) and into deposit-based accounts (TESSAs, cash, ISAs, high-interest savings accounts) to minimise the risk of short-term losses from the stockmarket.

○ Decide at retirement whether you wish to keep your capital invested, or to use it to buy an annuity which supplements the annuity from your main pension scheme.

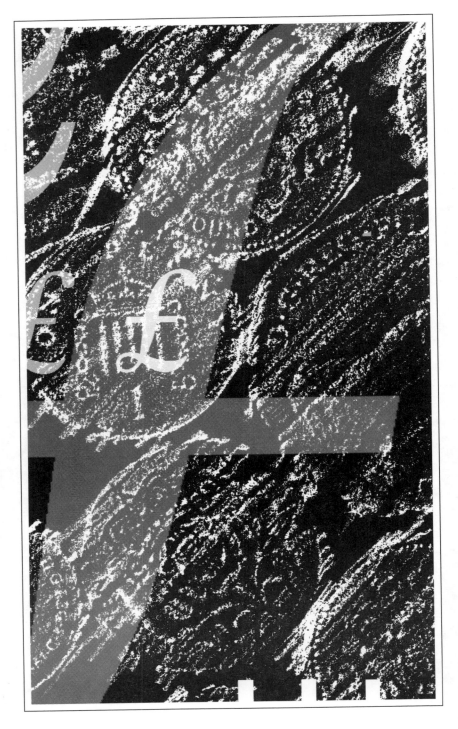

16 Taking your pension

Finally, all your planning and investment is about to come to fruition. After years of working and contributing to your pension, you can retire and start to enjoy yourself. But before that can happen there is still some planning to do and decisions to make.

Countdown to retirement

Your state pension The DSS should normally send you a claim form BR1 about four months before your state retirement age. If you do not receive one, contact your local Benefits Agency.

You have the choice of taking your pension at state retirement age, or of deferring it for up to five years. If you choose the option of deferring your state pension, you will earn increases to the pension of about 7·5% for each year you defer. After 6 April 2010, these increases will be at a rate of approximately 10·4% a year.

If you wish to defer taking your state pension, complete form BR432, which you will find in leaflet NI92 'Giving up your Retirement Pension to earn extra' from your local Benefits Agency.

FINAL SALARY EMPLOYERS PENSION SCHEMES

If you are a member of a final salary employers pension scheme, you should expect to receive a statement from your scheme about three months before your retirement date. This will state how much your pension should be. If you do not receive this statement, contact your pension scheme administrator. In situations where you have a preserved pension, make sure that the pension scheme knows how to get in touch with you. If the company has moved, and you do not know how to get in touch with it, contact the Pension Schemes Registry for help; they will send you a form (PR4) to fill in.

When you have received details of your benefits under your company scheme, you will need to supply the administrators with basic information such as details of the bank or building society account into which you would like your pension to be paid. You will probably also have to make the decision at this stage about whether to take a lump sum (see page 191); this will be true for most schemes. However, some do not offer lump sums, and with others, such as public sector schemes, the lump sum is given automatically.

Most people will take the lump sum. But be careful – if you are planning to use the lump sum for a specific purchase, such as a new house or car, or a cruise around the world, be sure that you do not reduce your remaining pension below the level you can afford to live on.

If you calculate that your remaining pension will be adequate after taking the lump sum, this is usually the option to choose:

❍ The lump sum is tax free, whereas the pension you will surrender in return for the lump sum would be taxable.

❍ You could use the lump sum to buy a 'purchased life' annuity which would give you an income alongside your pension. Both are taxable, but the purchased life annuity bought with the lump sum will be taxed more favourably than the pension. Part of the income from the purchased life annuity is treated as a return of the capital which was used in buying the annuity – and this part of the income is tax free.

Another important consideration is the effect taking a lump sum may have on a survivor pension. If you take a lump sum, any survivor pension would be reduced by the same proportion as your pension. Make sure that you are leaving your spouse, partner or dependent children enough to live on before you decide to take the lump sum.

Another decision your scheme may allow you to make is to take a smaller pension yourself from the outset, in return for providing a larger survivor pension when you die. It is worth considering this if you are in ill health and do not expect to live long in retirement; by taking a smaller pension yourself, you may be able to provide a better pension for your survivors.

MONEY PURCHASE EMPLOYERS PENSION SCHEMES

If you are in a money purchase scheme, procedures and the paperwork are very similar to a personal pension (see right). You will have the same choices to make about the lump sum (see page 191), and in addition you will have to decide on the type of annuity you wish to take – details of this are covered in 'Choosing your annuity', which you will find on page 193.

Personal pension plan members now have the option of deferring buying the annuity, and drawing income from the pension fund instead. This is designed to allow you to buy the annuity at a time when rates are favourable. Money purchase pension schemes do not yet have this option. The Government has indicated, however, that it intends to introduce such an option for money purchase plans. In the interim, if your scheme is an insured money purchase scheme (see Chapter 7), there is a temporary facility which you can use to withdraw income from the fund, without buying an annuity.

Independent financial adviser and *Moneywise* Ask the Professionals panellist Keith Sanham says:

"Annuities can be bought only from approved life insurance companies. It is a competitive marketplace and there are complex reasons why a particular company would decide to be in or out of the market. Specialist advice is absolutely essential to bring the best return for your investment."

PERSONAL PENSIONS

Your pension providers will contact you approximately two weeks before your retirement date. They will send you a statement indicating the value of your pension fund, and will also indicate the value of the provider's own annuity, based on standard assumptions for your gender and age (see page 193).

You have a number of choices that affect the nature of the pension you can enjoy:

O Do you want increases in your pension?
O Do you want your survivors to have a pension?
O Do you want the pension to be guaranteed for a certain length of time?

With most personal pension plans, you also have an 'open market option', which allows you to buy your annuity from any provider, not only the one with which you have invested over the years. This is a very valuable option, and you should make sure that it is available when you are buying a pension plan.

Although you will have specified a retirement date when you took out your personal pension, it is possible to retire earlier than this date. Your pension provider may impose a penalty on this – check when you buy the pension in the first place. If you want to retire earlier than this date, contact your provider about a month before you want to retire, in order to start the ball rolling.

189

Pension increases in retirement

Whilst you are working, you expect your salary to increase each year in line with the cost of living. The same should be true of a pension. Inflation – even at the relatively low levels of recent years – will soon eat into its purchasing power. The longer you live, the more inflation will erode your real income – as we discussed in Chapter 2.

Until recently, the only stipulation made by the Inland Revenue for increases to pensions related to those contracted out of SERPS – either through their company scheme or a personal pension. The Inland Revenue considers part of your pension to be the equivalent of what you would have received had you stayed in SERPS. It may not be exactly equivalent – this depends on the type of scheme.

The rules for each type of scheme identify that part of your pension:

○ If you're a member of a final salary employers pension scheme, then that part of your pension is known either as a Guaranteed Minimum Pension (for pension entitlements built up before April 1997) or as Requisite Benefit (for entitlements built up after April 1997). The Guaranteed Minimum Pension has to accumulate on the same terms as the SERPS pension would have done if you had still been contracted in. The new Requisite Benefit means that your protected SERPS equivalent pension must be worth at least 1/80 of 90% of your middle band earnings for each year of service. This is actually a higher amount than the GMP it replaces.

○ If you're a member of a money purchase employers scheme, or have a personal pension, the system is different. With both of these pension arrangements, you are building up an investment fund, which eventually pays for your pension. The part of that fund which is paid for by the rebates on National Insurance contributions – paid to your pension fund by the DSS because you are contracted out – is accumulated separately. This part of the fund is called Protected Rights and is subject to different conditions at retirement from the rest of your pension.

  • NB Some money purchase schemes are set up to contract out on the basis of Guaranteed Minimum Pension – check to see if this is the case with your scheme.

Regardless of the type of scheme, the SERPS-related part of your pension – Guaranteed Minimum Pension, Requisite Benefit or Protected Rights – has to increase as follows:

○ For entitlements which you built up prior to April 1997, the pension paid must increase by the full RPI each year.
○ For entitlements built up after April 1997, the pension paid must increase either by the RPI or by 5% – whichever is the lower. All of this increase is paid for by the pension scheme.

Remember – these requirements apply only to that part of your pension which is considered to be the equivalent of the pension you would have received if you were still contracted into SERPS.

Increases in the remainder of the pension you receive on retirement depend on the type of pension you have, except in the case of final salary schemes.

For a final salary scheme, there is a new requirement. Pension entitlements built up after April 1997 have to increase the whole pension, not just the SERPS-related part, by RPI or by 5% (if lower). Entitlements built up before April 1997 are increased at the scheme's discretion. Your pension scheme handbook should set out the scheme's normal policy – usually a fixed percentage increase. Few schemes automatically offer full indexation against RPI.

If you are in a money purchase scheme or have a personal pension, any increases in that part of your pension over and above the Protected Rights depend on the type of annuity you purchase.

Should you take the lump sum?

If your scheme lets you take a lump sum, you need to consider whether to take it. It is important to remember that taking a lump sum will reduce the size of the pension you can take, so you have to be sure that the reduced pension will be enough for you to live on.

In addition, you cannot reduce your pension below the level of the pension which is protected under the rules for contracting out of SERPS (see Chapters 6 and 7). The calculation for working out how much your pension will be reduced by after you take a lump sum is complicated, and will be performed by your pension scheme administrators. As a rough guide, if you are a man of 65, then for each £9 you take as a lump sum, your pension is likely to reduce by £1 a year. For a woman of 60, the pension reduces by £1 a year for each £11 she takes in a lump sum.

Remember that these figures are rough guides, and that they vary according to age and circumstances; they are also affected by the nature of the scheme to which you belong. It is, therefore, always best to obtain a forecast from your pension scheme administrator.

When you retire you will need to decide whether or not to take the lump sum option if your scheme offers it. You cannot decide later, once you have started receiving your pension. The decision largely depends on what you want to do with the money. If you have a need for capital – for buying a holiday home, a new car or paying for a world cruise for example – or if you want to invest the money for your children or grandchildren, then taking the lump sum can be a sensible option.

However, if your only plan for the lump sum is to supplement your pension income, then you are likely to be better off taking the larger pension instead of the lump sum. You are unlikely, in any circumstances, to be able to generate enough investment income from the lump sum to compensate for the pension you have given up – unless you use the lump sum to buy an annuity. The most important consideration of all is, of course, whether you can afford to live on a reduced pension if you decide to take the lump sum.

> **Example**
> You are a man of 65 retiring on a final salary of £18,000 and maximum pension entitlements. Therefore you are entitled to a maximum pension of £12,000 – two-thirds of your final salary – but you have the option of taking a lump sum tax free of up to 1.5 times your final salary – a maximum lump sum of £27,000.
> Using the rough guideline of losing £1 of pension a year for each £9 you take in the lump sum, you would reduce your annual pension by £27,000/9 – or £3,000 a year – so your pension falls to only £9,000 a year.

> If you are approaching retirement and are uncertain about whether or not to take a lump sum, then you should seek advice from an independent financial adviser.

Choosing your annuity

If you have a personal pension, or you are a member of a money purchase pension scheme, you are required to use your pension fund to purchase an annuity. This type of annuity is known as a 'scheme' or 'compulsory' annuity.

An annuity is an insurance contract. In return for the capital in your pension fund, the insurance company promises to pay you an income for life. The amount you are paid depends on a range of factors (see below).

The best option when buying an annuity is to have an open market option (see page 189) from your provider, so that you can select your annuity from any provider in the market. To do this, you may well want to use the services of an independent financial adviser .

Annuity rates are calculated on the basis of your age and sex, and your general state of health at the time. The rate that you are offered reflects the insurance company's calculations of:

○ How long it expects you to live. It is committing itself to pay you an income for the remainder of your life.
○ The features you want from your annuity, and particularly whether you want to fund survivor pensions. In this case, there is an open-ended commitment by the insurer for more than just your lifetime.
○ The investment gains it can expect from your pension fund. It will be the profits derived from this investment that help fund your income.

Annuity rates for women are lower than those for men, and this is because women, generally, have a longer average life expectancy than men.

If you are in poor health, or you are a smoker, then you may find that you are offered a favourable annuity rate, because the insurance company's actuary has calculated your life expectancy to be poor!

There are a range of options that you can choose when buying your annuity; for example you can opt for regular increases and to provide an income for dependants on your death Here are some options.

GUARANTEED ANNUITY

This type of annuity will pay the income promised for a specified period – usually five or ten years. If you die during that period, the income will continue to be paid to your survivors or estate. If you are alive at the end of the guarantee period, the annuity will continue to pay you the same income for the rest of your life, but the payments will cease on death once the guarantee period is over.

Without this type of guarantee, you could lose everything in your pension fund if you die the day after buying your annuity because it is the fund itself which is used to pay for the annuity. A guarantee is a way of making sure that you get a specified amount back from the fund.

Like all features which are added to the basic annuity, having a guarantee will reduce the rate at which the annuity pays you an income.

FUNDING A SURVIVOR PENSION

This can be achieved by taking out a joint life annuity, which will pay an income until both you and your partner die. A basic annuity would cover your life only. Again, the cost of the additional protection for your partner will mean a lower income from the annuity from the outset.

PROTECTING YOURSELF AGAINST INFLATION

A basic annuity will be level – the income payable remains the same for the rest of your life. If you live a long time, then inflation will erode the purchasing power of that income, so that the older you get, the poorer you become. If you are in poor health and do not expect to live long, this may not concern you. But if you expect to have a long and healthy retirement, you should consider an increasing annuity. With this type of annuity the income will go up each year, either by a fixed percentage (perhaps 3% or 5%), or by the full increase in the RPI. Again, choosing to protect your income with an increasing annuity will mean that your income is lower from the start. Full protection against changes in the RPI will also cost more than a modest fixed increase.

OTHER ANNUITY OPTIONS

You will also need to choose how frequently your annuity is paid – monthly, quarterly or annually – and also whether it is paid in advance or in arrears. All of these options again affect the annuity rate you will be paid, on the basis that the longer the insurance company has that capital to invest, the better gain it can make from it. So an annuity payable annually in arrears will offer a more favourable rate of income than an annuity payable monthly in advance.

Before deciding on this, be sure that you have the necessary 'float' to keep going until the first annuity payment is made, and if you choose quarterly or annual payments be certain that you will manage your income successfully over the period it is meant to last.

The different payment methods can have a big impact on your pension:

○ A pension paid monthly will be about 7% less than one paid annually.
○ A pension paid annually in advance will be about 15% less than one paid annually in arrears.

If you choose an annuity payable in arrears, be aware of what will happen if you die halfway between your pension payments. With some annuities, your estate will be paid the relevant portion of the pension due to you; with others, your estate forfeits any right to that income.

DEFERRING YOUR ANNUITY PURCHASE

With both personal pensions and money purchase occupational pensions, the actual pension paid to the member depends on the annuity which can be bought at the time of taking the proceeds of the pension scheme.

As mentioned before, an annuity is essentially an insurance policy – in return for the capital in your pension fund, the annuity will pay you an income for life. The size of that income depends on the investment returns which the provider expects to make from your capital. This is reflected in the interest rate which the annuity pays.

The problem with this system is that annuities, like other investments, suffer at times of poor investment growth. So, for example, during a recession investment growth will be poor, and providers of annuities will reduce their interest rates in exactly the same way that your bank will reduce interest on savings accounts if it cannot see a way of affording to pay that interest.

Whereas a bank can put up the interest again on your savings account, the interest rate on an annuity is fixed at the time it is sold. This is because of the complex actuarial calculations which have to be made at the time, which take into account your life expectancy and predict the length of time over which the annuity has to be paid. Increasing the interest rate at a later date could be too expensive for the provider – an annuity is an open-ended commitment, remember, since it has to be paid until you die.

If you retired and had to buy the annuity at once, then you could effectively find yourself having to take 'pot luck' with the interest rates which are current at that time. You could be lucky and retire at a point when interest rates are high; equally you could be unlucky and retire at the depths of a slump, and suffer a reduced income for the rest of your life.

To help pensioners avoid this 'lottery', the government introduced a new provision for personal pensions in the 1995 Pensions Act. It also indicated that it would introduce a similar provision for money purchase pension schemes; at the moment, only insured money purchase schemes have a temporary option which has the same effect (see page 96).

When your personal pension matures, you can defer buying the annuity. Instead, you can withdraw an income from the pension fund itself, until you decide to buy the annuity.

These deferral rules apply only to personal pensions. If you hold a retirement annuity contract, it cannot be deferred. You must buy the annuity at the time the retirement annuity contract matures.

Under the new deferral rules, you can defer buying the annuity and still take the lump sum at once. This is limited to a maximum of 25% of the fund and is tax free. If you defer buying your annuity, the fund – the reduced fund if you have taken a lump sum – continues to be invested on your behalf, and you can take an income from it. There are limits on the maximum and the minimum income you can withdraw each year:

○ The maximum limit is based on the annuity rates prevailing at the time. Specifically, the rate for a level annuity is used – one with no increases in future income – for the individual's age and gender, and paid monthly in arrears. They assume no dependant's pension and no guaranteed period of payment. This form of annuity would offer the highest interest rate to the individual at the time.
○ The minimum level of income is 35% of the maximum level.
○ This income level has to be reviewed every three years in line with the annuity rates prevailing at the time.

If you have set your personal pension up as a series of separate policies within the overall plan (see Chapter 10, page 131), each segment can be treated separately for deferral purposes. If you defer buying the annuity, you can decide to buy at any stage up to your 75th birthday, at which stage you have to make a purchase.

If you die while having deferred buying an annuity, your spouse or dependant(s) have the following options:

Warning

It is extremely important that you are aware of the risks of deferring buying your annuity, if you think this is the course of action for you:

○ There is absolutely no guarantee that annuity interest rates will improve during the period of deferring your purchase; they may well get worse.

○ While you defer, your pension fund continues to be invested on your behalf, so there are risks of the investment itself losing value, due to a stockmarket crash, for example.

○ Withdrawing income from the pension fund carries the danger of depleting it so much that the remaining fund is too small to buy a worthwhile annuity.

The option to defer your annuity purchase has the potential to provide you with a higher pension than you could have received at the time your pension plan matures, but it is essential that you have considered all the risks, and are comfortable with your decision. If you have any doubt about the best course of action, consult a qualified independent financial adviser.

○ Your spouse or dependant can continue to draw an income from the fund in the same way you did, until the earlier of either their 75th birthday or the date you would have reached 75. In this case the maximum and minimum income levels are calculated according to the spouse or dependant's age and gender, but with the additional qualification that the maximum cannot exceed the maximum you could have been paid if the calculation had been made the day before you died.

○ Your spouse or dependant can buy an annuity in the usual way.

○ He or she can take your pension fund as a lump sum – with a liability to tax, which is currently at a rate of 35%.

The biggest danger of pension drawdown is that of depleting the pension fund so far that you will be unable to buy a good pension, even if annuity rates improve. The continued investment of the fund will probably not compensate for the income withdrawn, with the result that your residual fund will become smaller (see page 130 for a flowchart demonstrating the effect).

The advantage is that if you die before buying your annuity, your pension fund will be available to your estate. The estate will be liable to inheritance tax on the fund. If you are in ill health and do not expect to live long, then drawdown is a useful option because your pension fund will pass to your estate on death.

STAGGERED RETIREMENT
If you have set up your personal pension plan as a series of segmented smaller plans (see Chapter 10), then you can phase your retirement by cashing in segments at different times to buy annuities. This allows you a certain amount of flexibility, and could mean that you're better off in the long run – cashing in more segments to increase your pension, while winding down work slowly.

Independent financial adviser and *Moneywise* Ask the Professionals panellist Rebekah Kearey says:

"This is a complex area where the liberal sprinkling of rules and regulations constrict the assumptions that must be made about the future. Consult a professional to choose the best course of action."

Tax when you take your pension

At retirement you will usually have the option of taking a lump sum of up to 1·5 times your final salary (employers pension scheme) or up to 25% of the fund. This sum is tax free.

The annuity you buy with your pension fund is liable to income tax in the normal way. Income from your pension will be aggregated together with any other income you receive, including any State pension. You can offset your personal allowance(s) (see Chapter 3) against this total, in order to calculate your taxable income.

The basic state pension is normally paid gross. If it is your only income, your personal allowances will usually mean that you have no tax liability at all. If you have other income and are therefore liable to tax, the state pension will still usually be paid gross, and the tax you have to pay will be deducted via PAYE from your company or personal pension.

A pension from your company scheme or a personal pension is usually paid net of tax, which is deducted through PAYE. The rate of tax may look too high; this may be because the tax liability on the state pension is being collected via the PAYE system.

Remember that your personal allowances increase once you are aged over 65, and again over 75, but there is an earnings limit and income over that limit will reduce your age-related personal allowances by £1 for every £2 of income over the limit. However, this procedure cannot reduce your personal allowances to less than the normal allowance for someone under 65 (see Chapter 3).

Action plan

○ In the run-up to retirement, be aware of what information you should be receiving from the State and from your company scheme or personal pension. If you have not received this information, contact the necessary people and inform them.

○ If you wish to defer taking your state pension, notify the DSS as soon as possible after receiving its notification of your pension.

○ Be clear about the options you want for your pension, especially the lump sum you wish to take, and your provision for survivor pensions.

○ With a personal pension, use the open market option (if available to you) to choose the best annuity on the market.

○ Decide on the features you need from your annuity, and obtain quotations which indicate the costs to your pension of those features.

○ Consider your options for deferring your pension. Consult an independent financial adviser if you have any doubts about what to do.

Finally, once you have made all the decisions and completed all the paperwork, all that remains is to relax, and reap the benefits of all those years of planning your pension.

Enjoy your retirement!

An A-Z guide to financial words and phrases

Accrual rate The rate at which pension entitlement builds up. Often expressed as a fraction of your final salary for each year served, for example 1/60, 1/80. Can be used to refer to Inland Revenue limits on how a pension entitlement builds up. Also can refer to the actual pension entitlement built up for each year of membership of a final salary company pension scheme.

Additional voluntary contributions (AVCs) Extra payments paid into company pension schemes by members to improve their benefits.

Annual percentage rate (APR) The real cost, in terms of interest and fees, of credit (used for comparison purposes).

Annuity A form of income bought through insurance companies with the proceeds from a pension fund, which pays a guaranteed sum throughout your lifetime.

Base rate The interest rate set by the Bank of England, used as a basis for the rates that banks offer their customers.

Basic state pension Flat rate pension payable to all individuals who have made sufficient National Insurance contributions.

Bid-to-offer spread The difference between the price at which investments can be bought and the price at which they can then be sold.

Bond A certificate of debt issued by companies and governments to raise cash, usually paying interest and traded in a market.

Capital gains tax (CGT) The tax payable on profits from the sale of assets, particularly shares.

Contracting out A legal arrangement under which you can give up part of your SERPS benefits and build up an equivalent or better benefit in a company scheme or personal pension.

Convertible A security, usually a bond or debenture issued by a company, that can be converted into the ordinary shares or preference shares of that company at a fixed date or dates, and at a fixed price.

Deed of covenant A promise made in a deed, often used as a means of providing funds to charities or to transfer income from one person to another, with a view to saving tax.

Derivative A financial instrument that is valued according to the expected price movements of an underlying asset, for example a share or a currency.

Dividend The distribution of part of the earnings of a company to its shareholders

Earnings per share (EPS) The earnings of a company over a stated period, usually a year, divided by the number of ordinary shares it has issued.

Endowment policy A life insurance and savings policy which pays a specified amount of money on an agreed date, or on the death of the person insured, whichever is sooner.

Equities The ordinary shares of a publicly quoted company.

European Currency Unit (ECU) A form of currency calculated as a weighted average of a basket of EC currencies.

Final salary pension scheme a Company pension scheme in which your pension depends on your salary at retirement, your number of years' service, and the fraction of final salary awarded for each year's service, for example 1/60.

Financial Services Authority (FSA) The main body responsible for regulating the way investments, including pensions, are run and sold.

Free-standing additional voluntary contributions (FSAVCs) Extra payments made to boost a pension by investing with an insurance company, not an employers scheme. See 'AVCs'.

Friendly Society A mutual organisation offering tax-free investment plans with a life-insurance element, normally over ten years.

Fund A reserve of money or investments held for a specific purpose – for example, to be divided into units for investors to buy (as in a unit trust fund) or to provide a pension income (as in a pension fund).

Future A contract to buy or sell a fixed number of commodities, currencies, or shares at a fixed date in the future at a fixed price.

Gearing The ratio of the amount of long-term loans and preference shares to ordinary shares in a company.

Gilt-edged security (gilt) A fixed-interest security issued by the British Government.

Guaranteed income bond (GIB) A bond guaranteeing the full return of capital plus a fixed income, issued by life insurance companies.

Held in trust An arrangement allowing property or cash to be held by a trustee on behalf of a named beneficiary.

Independent financial adviser (IFA) An adviser committed to offering 'best advice' on the range of investments and plans in the marketplace, not someone selling investments from just one company.

Individual Savings Account (ISA) Available from April 1999, a plan used to hold bank and building society accounts, National Savings, life insurance and share-based investments with any income and capital gains free of tax.

Inheritance tax (IHT) A form of wealth tax on inherited money: £223,000 can be inherited before this tax is incurred.

Initial charge The charge paid to the managers of a unit trust by an investor when he or she first buys units – usually between 3% and 5%.

Investment trust A company quoted on the stock exchange which invests in other companies' shares.

Lower earnings limit (LEL) Weekly wage roughly equivalent to the basic state pension. If you earn less than this amount, you do not pay National Insurance contributions. If you earn more that the LEL, your earnings up to the upper earnings limit (UEL) are liable to National Insurance contributions. Earnings between the LEL and the UEL are called middle band earnings.

Middle band earnings Earnings between the lower and upper earnings limits. The SERPS pension relates to these earnings.

Money purchase pension scheme A company pension scheme in which your pension is dependent on the amount paid into the pension fund, and the investment performance of that fund.

Mortgage interest relief at source (MIRAS) Tax relief at 10% on the interest on the first £30,000 borrowed to buy a house.

National Insurance contributions Contributions payable on earnings if you earn more than the lower earnings limit, to pay for state benefits and pensions.

Negative equity The condition whereby the current market value of a house is worth less than the amount outstanding on a mortgage.

Net relevant earnings Earnings from self-employment or employment which are used to calculate the maximum payments into a personal pension.

Nominees Individuals or companies which hold shares on behalf of investors, to reduce the costs of administering a portfolio, or to conceal the true owners of the shares.

Offshore funds Funds based outside the UK for tax reasons.

Open market option The right to use a pension fund on retirement to buy an annuity from any insurance company, not just the provider of the pension plan.

Option A contract giving the right (but not the obligation) to buy or sell commodities, currencies or shares at a fixed date in the future at a fixed price.

Pay as you earn (PAYE) The system whereby employers collect tax from employees and pass it on to the Inland Revenue.

Penny shares Securities with a very low market price – investors usually hope for rapid recoveries or takeovers.

201

Pensionable earnings
Earnings on which pension benefits and/or contributions are calculated.

Pensionable service The length of time in a particular job which qualifies for pension benefit. Usually this equates to the length of time as a member of the pension scheme.

Pension transfer A payment made from one pension scheme to another, or to an insurance company running a personal pension scheme to fund a buy-out scheme. Enables pension rights to be moved out of the pension scheme of a previous employer.

Permanent health insurance (PHI) Insurance which replaces income lost due to long-term illness or injury and pays benefits relative to the size of a salary.

Personal allowances Amounts of income which you are allowed tax free.

Personal equity plan (PEP) A plan used to hold UK shares, unit trusts, investment trusts, and now corporate bonds, with any dividends and capital gains free of tax.

Personal pension plan An approved scheme for people who are self-employed or not in a company scheme. Personal pensions are arranged through insurance companies, and are individual money purchase schemes.

Preserved pensions Pension rights built up in a pension scheme, which have been left in that scheme when you ceased employment with that company.

Price/earnings ratio (P/E ratio) The market price of a company share divided by the earnings per share of that company.

Retail price index (RPI) The official measure of inflation calculated by weighting the costs of goods and services to approximate a typical family spending pattern.

Retirement annuity contract A type of personal pension superseded in 1988 by personal pensions themselves.

Rights issue New shares sold by a company to raise new capital.

Scrip issue The issue of new share certificates to existing shareholders to reflect an accumulation of profits on the balance sheet.

Self-invested personal pension (SIPP) A personal pension under which the member has the ability to control the investments.

Share An investment in and part ownership of a company, conferring the right to part of the company's profits (usually by payment of a dividend), and to any voting rights attached to that share, and which, in the case of public companies, can be traded on the open market.

Split-capital investment trust A limited-life investment trust in which the equity capital is divided into income shares and capital shares.

State earnings-related pension scheme (SERPS) A state pension in addition to the basic state pension, plus widows' benefits and invalidity benefits, based on earnings.

Stockmarket A market for the buying and selling of shares and securities.

Tax-exempt special savings accounts (TESSAs) Five-year savings accounts which are exempt from tax, and available from banks and building societies.

Tax year The tax system works on the basis of tax years which run from 6 April one calendar year to 5 April the next.

Term assurance or insurance Life insurance with no investment element.

Unit-linked policy An insurance policy in which the benefits depend on the performance of units in a fund invested in shares or property.

Unit trust A pooled fund of stockmarket investments divided into equal units.

Upper earnings limit The maximum weekly wage above which there is no liability to National Insurance contributions.

Value-added tax (VAT) A form of indirect taxation borne by traders and consumers, levied on goods and services.

Whole-of-life policy A life insurance policy which pays a specified amount on the death of the life insured.

With-profits policy A life insurance or pension policy with additional amounts added to the sum insured.

Yield The income from an investment.

Zero-rated Goods or services that are liable to VAT, but with a tax rate of zero.

Directory

REGULATORY BODIES

Financial Servies Authority (FSA)
Formerly Securities and Investments Board (SIB)
Gavrelle House, 2-14 Bunhill Row, London EC1Y 8RA
0171 638 1240
Register of advisers
0171 390 5000

Investment Managers Regulatory Organisation (IMRO)
Lloyds Chambers, 1 Portsoken Street, London E1 8BT
0171 390 5000

Investors' Compensation Scheme (ICS)
Gavrelle House, 2-14 Bunhill Row, London EC1Y 8RA
0171 638 1240

The Office of the Investment Ombudsman
6 Frederick's Place, London EC2R 8BT
0171 769 3065

Personal Investment Authority (PIA)
1 Canada Square, Canary Wharf, London E14 5AZ
0171 538 8860

Securities and Futures Authority Ltd (SFA)
Cotton Centre, Cottons Lane, London SE1 2QB
0171 378 9000

SAVINGS AND INVESTMENTS

Association of Investment Trust Companies (AITC)
Durrant House, 8-13 Chiswell Street, London EC1Y 4YY
0171 588 5347

Association of Policy Market Makers
Holywell Centre, 1 Phipp Street, London EC2A 4PS
0171 739 3949
(for a list of companies selling second-hand endowments)

Association of Solicitor Investment Managers (ASIM)
Baldocks, Chiddingstone Cause, Tonbridge, Kent TN11 8JX
01892 870065

Association of Unit Trusts and Investment Funds (AUTIF)
Information Unit, 65 Kingsway, London WC2B 6TD
0171 831 0898

National Savings Information
Room 073, Charles House, 376 Kensington High Street, London W14 8SD
0645 645000

ProShare
Library Chambers, 13-14 Basinghall Street, London EC2V 5BQ
0171 600 0984

Stock Exchange
Old Broad Street, London EC2N 1HP
0171 588 2355

BANKS AND BUILDING SOCIETIES

British Bankers' Association
105-108 Old Broad Street London EC2N 1EX
0171 216 8800

Banking Ombudsman
70 Grays Inn Road, London WC1X 8NB
0171 404 9944

Building Societies Association
3 Savile Row, London W1X 1AF
0171 437 0655

Council of Mortgage Lenders
3 Savile Row, London W1X 1AF
0171 437 0075

Building Societies Ombudsman
Millbank Tower, Millbank, London SW1P 4XS
0171 931 0044

PENSIONS

Association of Consulting Actuaries (ACA)
1 Wardrobe Place,
London EC4V 5AH
0171 248 3163

Association of Consulting Actuaries (ACA)
1 Wardrobe Place, London EC4V 5AH
0171 248 3163

Occupational Pensions Advisory Service (OPAS)
11 Belgrave Road,
London SW1V 1RB
0171 233 8080

Pensions Ombudsman
11 Belgrave Road,
London SW1V 1RB
0171 834 9144

CREDIT REFERENCE AGENCIES

Experian (formerly CCN group)
Consumer Help Service,
PO Box 8000, Nottingham NG1 25GX
0115 976 8747

Equifax Europe Ltd
Department 1E, PO Box 3001,
Glasgow, G81 2DT
0990 783783

FINANCIAL ADVICE

Independent Financial Advice Promotion (IFAP)
4th Floor, 28 Greville Street,
London EC1N 8SU
0117 971 1177
(for a list of three independent advisers in your area)

Institute of Financial Planning
Whitefriars Centre,
Lewins Mead, Bristol BS1 2NT
0117 930 4434

TAX AND ACCOUNTANCY

Chartered Association of Certified Accountants (CACA)
29 Lincoln's Inn Fields,
London WC2A 3EE
0171 242 6855

Inland Revenue
Somerset House,
London WC2R 1LB
0171 438 6420
(or look in the phone book for your local tax office)

Institute of Chartered Accountants in England and Wales (ICAEW)
Chartered Accountants Hall,
PO Box 433, Moorgate Place,
London EC2P 2BJ
0171 920 8100

Institute of Chartered Accountants in Scotland (ICAS) 27 Queen Street,
Edinburgh EH2 1LA
0131 225 5673

TaxAid
342 Kilburn High Road,
London NW6 2QJ
0171 624 3768 (9am-11am)
(for free tax advice)

INSURANCE

Association of British Insurers (ABI)
51 Gresham Street,
London EC2V 7HQ
0171 600 3333

British Investment Insurance Brokers Association (BIIBA)
14 Bevis Marks,
London EC3A 7NT
0171 623 9043

Insurance Brokers Registration Council (IBRC)
63 St Mary Axe,
London EC3A 8NB
0171 621 1061

Insurance Ombudsman Bureau
City Gate One,
135 Park Street,
London SE1 9EA
0171 928 4488

LAW

Law Society
113 Chancery Lane,
London WC2A 1PL
0171 242 1222

Law Society of Scotland
26 Drumsheugh Gardens,
Edinburgh EH3 7YR
0131 226 7411

Legal Services Ombudsman
22 Oxford Court,
Oxford Street,
Manchester M2 3WQ
0161 236 9532

Office for the Supervision of Solicitors
Victoria Court, 8 Dormer Place,
Leamington Spa,
Warwickshire CV32 5AE
01926 820082

CONSUMER AFFAIRS

Citizens Advice Bureau (CAB)
Myddleton House, 115-123
Pentonville Road, London N1 9LZ
0171 833 2181 (or look in the phone book)

Consumers' Association
2 Marylebone Road,
London NW1 4DF
0171 830 6000

Help the Aged
St James's Walk,
London EC1R 0BE
0171 253 0253

Money Advice Association
1st Floor, Gresham House,
24 Holborn Viaduct,
London EC1A 2BN
0171 236 3566

National Debtline
318 Summer Lane,
Birmingham B19 3RL
0121 359 8501

National Gas Consumers Council
6th Floor, Abford House,
15 Wilton Road,
London SW1V 1LT
0171 931 0977

Office of Electricity Regulation (OFFER)
Hagley House, Hagley Road,
Edgbaston B16 8QG
0121 456 2100

Office of Fair Trading (OFT)
Field House,
15-25 Bream's Buildings,
London EC4A 1PR
0171 242 2858

Office of Gas Supply (OFGAS)
130 Wilton Road,
London SW1V 1LQ
0171 828 0898

Office of Telecommunications Services (OFTEL)
Export House,
50 Ludgate Hill,
London EC4M 7JJ
0345 145000

Office of Water Services (OFWAT)
Centre City Tower,
7 Hill Street,
Birmingham B5 4UA
0121 625 1300

Trading Standards Coordinating Body
PO Box 6, Fell Road,
Croydon CR9 1LG
0181 688 1996
(or look in the phone book for your local office)

BENEFITS

Age Concern
Astral House, 1268 London
Road, London SW16 4ER
0181 679 8000
(or look in the phone book for your local office)

Benefits Agency
Look in the phone book under
Benefits Agency or DSS.

Disability Benefits
The Benefit Enquiry Line is
open for people with disabilities
and their carers
0800 882200

National Association for Widows
54-57 Allison Street, Digbeth,
Birmingham B5 5TH
0121 643 8348

Office of Social Security Commissioners
83-86 Farringdon Street,
London EC4A 1PR
0171 353 5145

Department of Social Security (DSS)
Richmond House, Whitehall,
London SW1A 2NS
0171 210 3000 (or look in the
phone book for your local office).

Index

accelerated accrual, employers pensions 60, 62
ACT (advance corporation tax) 33-34, 41, 58
action plans
checking progress 167
employers pensions 79, 103
final salary schemes 87
financial advisers 159
money purchase schemes 97
moving jobs 111
personal pension choices 147
personal pensions 137
retirement lifestyle 35
savings/investments utilization 185
state pensions 55
taking pensions 199
tax and National Insurance 43
topping up pensions 177
actuaries 65-67, 72, 109
additional personal allowances 54
additional voluntary contributions (AVCs) 29, 42, 170-173, 200
advance corporation tax (ACT) 33-34, 41, 58
advisers
financial advisers
age related rebates 128
annual reports
final salary schemes 163-164
money purchase schemes 164-165
personal pensions 165-167
annuities 183-184, 200
money purchase schemes 89-92
personal pensions 115-116
selection 193-198
annuity deferral 96, 189, 195-198
personal pensions 129, 131
warnings 197
appropriate personal pensions 127
AVCs (additional voluntary contributions) 29, 42, 170-173, 200
basic details, pensions 15-17
basic state pensions 200
accessibility 48
drawbacks 14-15
forecasts 46, 49, 51, 161
maximization flowchart 19
outline 45-49
qualifications for 45-46
taxation 40-42, 48, 199
widows 54-55
worth 46-47
booklet, employers pensions 79, 81, 84, 90
boosting pension schemes 28
flowchart 20
BR1 forms 187
BR19 forms, pension forecasts

46, 49, 51, 161
BR432 forms 187
Budget (July 1997), pension changes 33-34, 41, 58, 128

carry forward/carry back, personal pensions 124, 174, 176-177
charges, personal pensions 145-147
checking progress, pensions 161-167
Christmas bonus 47
citizenship pensions 15
commission, financial advisers 153-154
company schemes
employers pensions
complaints, financial advisers 156-159
contracting out 43, 200
outline 51-53
personal pensions 52-53, 127
contributions
employers 65-67, 122
employers pensions 64-65, 170
group pensions 99-100
halting 84
pension advantages 33-34
personal pensions 117-122, 173-177
refunds 70, 106
tax relief 40, 57-58
contributions see also additional voluntary contributions; National Insurance
controlling directors
final salary 64
pension plans 100-101
credits, National Insurance contributions 45-46, 162

death in service
employers pensions 70-71
personal pensions 126
deferral, state pensions 187
deferral see also annuity deferral
defined benefit schemes
final salary schemes
defined contribution schemes
money schemes
dependants 69-70, 92
annuity deferral 196-197
personal pensions 125
discretionary increases, pension transfers 109
divorce, Pensions Act (1995) 34-35

early retirement
final salary schemes 84-85
money purchase schemes 93
personal pensions 116

early retirement voluntary 92-93
earnings cap 133, 134
employers pensions 63-64, 102
future threat 179
personal pensions 117, 118-119
topping up pensions 172-173
earnings limits 201, 202
National Insurance 43
state earnings-related pension scheme 50-51
employers contributions 65-67, 122
employers pensions 17, 134-137
additional voluntary contributions 170-173
benefits 67-69
contracting out 52-53
death in service 70-71
eligibility 77-78
employers contributions 65-67
final salary contributions 61-62, 64
importance 16
Inland Revenue rules 59-71
investments 73-77
lump sums 67-69
maximization flowchart 21
maximum contributions 65, 66, 170
maximum limits 61-65
outlines 57-79
progress checking 162, 165
protection 76-77
retirement age 60-61
running 71-77
survivor pensions 69-70, 71
taxation 57-58, 70, 197
topping up 170-173
transfers 105, 107-111
trusts 71-77
types 58, 99-103
unapproved schemes 102-03
employers pensions see also final salary schemes
executive pension plans 100-101
exempt approved pension schemes 57-58, 71
expenses analysis 26-28

fact-finding checklists, financial advisers 154-155
final salary calculations 62-64, 81-84
final salary schemes 58, 76-77, 81-87, 200
countdown 187-188
early retirement 84-85
final salary calculations 81-84
increases 190, 191
progress checking 162-164
public sector 85-86
transfers 109-110
Finance Act (1989) 102
financial advisers 149-159, 198

advice process 155-59
complaints 156-159
fact-find checklists 154-155
outline 149-151
payment methods 15, 154
qualifications 151, 152
questions checklist 151-154
Financial Services Act (1986) 149
Financial Services Authority
(FSA) 136, 150, 158
flowcharts
basic state pension
maximization 19
company scheme
maximization 21
pension scheme boosting 20
personal pension scheme
maximization 22
planning pensions 18
savings/investments utilization
23
forecasting pensions,
BR19 form 46, 49, 51, 161
free-standing additional voluntary
contributions (FSAVCs)
170-173, 201
fund managers 72, 74-75
funded unapproved retirement
benefit schemes (FURBs)
23, 103

group personal pensions 99-100
guaranteed annuity 194
guaranteed minimum pension
(GMP) 106, 107, 190-191

handbook, employers pensions
78, 79, 81, 84, 90
"headroom check" 172

illness, money purchase
schemes 93-95
income tax Inland Revenue;
taxation
independant advisers 151
Independant Financial Advice
Promotion (IFAP) 151
individual savings accounts (ISAs)
23, 182-183, 201, 23, 182-183,
201
inflation
basic state pension link 14, 47
earnings cap link 62-63, 119
effects 32
pension increases 190-191
protective annuities 194-195
public sector schemes 86
inheritance tax 197-198
Inland Revenue
communications 41-42
employers pensions 59-71
personal pensions 115-124
Inland Revenue see also taxation
Institute of Actuaries 109
insured money purchase
schemes 95-96
investment trusts 143, 201
investments
employers pensions 73-77

inflation effects 33
money purchase schemes 93
personal pensions 142-144
progress checking 163-167
utilization 179-184
utilization flowchart 23
investments see also savings

jobs
change of 105-111
multiple, personal pensions
119-120

"key features" documents 146

life expectancy
final salary schemes 85
improvements in 14, 15
lifestyle, retirement 25-35
limited prices index (LPI) 52
lower earnings limit (LEL) 43, 201
lump sums
annuity deferral 196, 197
decisive factors 191-192
employers pensions 67-69
final salary schemes 188
money purchase schemes 91-92
personal pensions 124
taxation benefits 192, 197

marginal rate tax relief,
personal pensions 120, 122
middle band earnings
earnings limits
Money Management 144, 166
money purchase schemes
58, 89-97, 201
annuities 90-91
benefits 91-92
countdown 188-189
early retirement 92-93
increases 190-191
investments 94-95
lump sums 91-92
mortgages, personal pensions
128-129
moving jobs 105-111
multiple jobs, personal pensions
119-120

National Insurance 201
basic state pension 15, 45-47
contracting out 43, 51-53,
127-128, 200
credits 45-46, 162
outline 42-43
voluntary contributions 162
net relevant earnings 117, 201

Occupational Pensions Advisory
Service (OPAS) 157
Occupational Pensions
Regulatory Authority (OPRA) 76
Ombudsman 157, 158
open market option 140, 157, 158,
193, 201

P2(T) forms 39
P9D forms 39

P11D forms 39, 62, 66, 121
P60 forms 38
payment methods,
financial advisers 153-154
payment options,
annuities 194-195
penalties, personal pension
transfers 146-147
pension fund changes, Budget
(July 1997) 33-34, 41, 58, 128
pension managers 72
pension transfers 105, 107-111,
146-147, 202
valuation calculations 108-109
Pensions Act (1995) 52
divorce 34-35
protection 67, 76-77
trusts 71, 72, 73
Pensions Ombudsman 157, 158
PEPs (personal equity plans)
179, 180-181, 202
person pensions
Inland Revenue rules 115-124
mis-selling (1988-94) 135-137
mortgages 128-129
multiple jobs 119-120
outline 113-115
progress checking 165-167
requirements checklist 140-141
retirement age 115-116
segmentation 131, 196, 198
selection 139-147
survivor pensions 125-126
target achievemenst 30-31
taxation 120, 122-123, 198-199
topping up 174-177
transfers 105, 107-111, 146-147
types 132-134
personal allowances 38-40, 202
personal equity plans (PEPs)
179, 180-181, 202
Personal Investment Authority
(PIA) 31, 150, 159
personal pensions 16, 17,
99-100, 113-137, 202
annuity deferral 129, 131
assessment 134-135
benefits 124-126
carry forward/carry back
124, 174, 176-177
charges 145-147
contracting out 52-53, 127
countdown 189
death in service 126
earnings cap 117, 118-119
eligibility 115
employers contributions 122
importance 16
increases 190-191
investment types 142-144
lump sums 124
maximization flowchart 22
maximum contributions
117-124, 173
maximum limits 116-117
PIA (Personal Investment
Authority) 16, 17, 99-100
Planned Savings 144, 166
planning, retirement 13-28

planning pensions, flowchart 18
PP42 forms 174
PP43 forms 176
PP120 forms 174, 176
preserved pensions 78, 105-107,
    109-110, 202
    countdown 187-188
progress checking, pensions
    161-167
protection, employers pensions
    65-67, 76-77
public sector pension schemes
    85-86
Public Sector Transfer Club 110
purchased life annuities 183-184

qualifications, financial advisers
    150-151, 152
question checklist, financial
    advisers 151-154

requirements checklist, personal
    pensions 140-141
Requisite Benefit 107, 190
Retail Price Index (RPI) inflation
retirement
    calculator examples 27, 28, 30, 31
    countdown 187-199
    lifestyle 25-35
    planning 13-23, 25-28
    savings/investments utilization
        23, 179-185
retirement age 84-85, 92-93
    employers pensions 60-61
    personal pensions 115-116
retirement annuity contracts
    113, 132-134, 202
review, pensions opt-outs
    (1988-94) 135137
risk profiles 154-155

savings
    pensions comparison 14, 32-34
    utilization 179-185
    utilization flowchart 23

savings *see also* investments
Section 32 "buy out" policies 107
segmented personal pensions
    131, 196, 197
self-invested personal pensions
    (SIPPs) 132, 202
SERPS state earnings-related
    pension scheme
small self-administered
schemes (SSAS) 101-102
stakeholder pensions 15
state earnings-related pension
    scheme (SERPS) 15, 43, 202
    benefits 50-51
    contracting out 43, 51-53,
        126-128
    outline 49-53
    personal pensions 126-128
    widows 54-55
state graduated pension scheme
    49
state pensions 45-55
    countdown 187
    deferral 187
    progress checking 161-162
state pensions *see also* basic
state pensions; state earnings-
    related pension scheme
stockmarket performance
    (1920-95) 144-145
survivor pensions
    employers pensions 69-70, 71
    funding 194
    money pension schemes 92
    personal pensions 125

target achievement table,
    personal pensions 30, 31
targeted money purchase
    schemes 94-95
tax year, definition 37, 202
tax-exempt special savings
    accounts (TESSAs) 23, 181-182,
    202
taxation 27-28

codes 38, 39
contribution refunds 106
contributions relief 40, 57-58
death in srvice 70
employers pension concessions
    57-58, 70
inheritances 197, 201
lump sums 192, 198
outline 37-42
pension receipts 40, 42, 48-49,
    198-199
personal equity plans
    179, 180-181
personal pensions relief 120,
    122, 123
rates 37, 40
reclamation 33-34, 41, 58
TESSAs (tax-exempt special
    savings accounts) 23, 181-182,
    202
tied agents 151
top-up pension schemes 102-103
topping up pensions 169-177
transferred pensions 105, 107-111,
    146-147
trusts
    definition 71, 73
    employers pensions 71-77

unapproved schemes, employers
    pensions 102-103
unfunded unapproved retirement
    benefit schemes (UURBS) 103
unit-linked policies 143-144, 202

voluntary early retirement 92-93

waiver of premium 140
widowers benefits 54
widows benefits 54-55
with profits insurance policies
    143-144, 202
working life, definition 45